Get Started in Creative Writing

Teach® Yourself

Get Started in Creative Writing

Stephen May

For UK order enquiries: please contact
Bookpoint Ltd, 130 Milton Park, Abingdon, Oxon OX14 4SB.
Telephone: +44 (0) 1235 827720. Fax: +44 (0) 1235 400454.
Lines are open 09.00–17.00, Monday to Saturday, with a 24-hour
message answering service. Details about our titles and how to
order are available at www.teachyourself.com

For USA order enquiries: please contact McGraw-Hill Customer
Services, PO Box 545, Blacklick, OH 43004-0545, USA.
Telephone: 1-800-722-4726. Fax: 1-614-755-5645.

For Canada order enquiries: please contact McGraw-Hill Ryerson Ltd,
300 Water St, Whitby, Ontario L1N 9B6, Canada.
Telephone: 905 430 5000. Fax: 905 430 5020.

Long renowned as the authoritative source for self-guided
learning – with more than 50 million copies sold worldwide –
the **Teach Yourself** series includes over 500 titles in the fields of
languages, crafts, hobbies, business, computing and education.

British Library Cataloguing in Publication Data:
a catalogue record for this title is available from the British Library.

Library of Congress Catalog Card Number: on file.

First published in UK 2008 by Hodder Education, part of
Hachette UK, 338 Euston Road, London, NW1 3BH.

First published in US 2010 by The McGraw-Hill Companies, Inc.

This edition published 2010.

Previously published as *Teach Yourself Creative Writing*.

The **Teach Yourself** name is a registered trade mark of
Hodder Headline.

Typeset by MPS Limited, a Macmillan Company.

Printed in Great Britain for Hodder Education, an Hachette UK
Company, 338 Euston Road, London NW1 3BH, by CPI Cox &
Wyman, Reading, Berkshire RG1 8EX.

The publisher has used its best endeavours to ensure that the URLs
for external websites referred to in this book are correct and active
at the time of going to press. However, the publisher and the
author have no responsibility for the websites and can make no
guarantee that a site will remain live or that the content will remain
relevant, decent or appropriate.

Hachette UK's policy is to use papers that are natural, renewable
and recyclable products and made from wood grown in sustainable
forests. The logging and manufacturing processes are expected to
conform to the environmental regulations of the country of origin.

Impression number   10 9 8 7 6 5 4 3 2

Year   2014 2013 2012 2011 2010

Acknowledgements

Warm thanks and appreciation to Camilla Hornby, Ilona Jones, Ariane Koek, Claire Macnamee, Caron May, Carol and Charles Ockleford, Victoria Roddam and all the writers who have helped contribute to this project.

The author and publisher are grateful to the following authors, publishers, agents and literary executors for permission to use copyright material: 'To Writing' by John Siddique, from THE PRIZE, published by Rialto © John Siddique, reprinted with kind permission of the author; professional tip by David Armstrong, reprinted with permission; professional tip by Anthony Clavane, reprinted with permission; extract from 'Capacity' from PORTRAIT OF MY MOTHER, WHO POSED NUDE IN WARTIME by Marjorie Sandor, published by Sarabande Books, Inc © 2003, reprinted by permission of Sarabande Books and the author; short extract from WHERE I'M CALLING FROM by Raymond Carver, published by Harvill Press © 1976, 1977, 1981, 1983, 1986, 1987, 1988, reprinted with permission of The Random House Group Ltd and Grove/Atlantic Inc; short extract from THINK LIKE A BEE by Jo Verity, Leaf Press, Cardiff, reprinted with permission of the author; exercise by Suzanne Berne, reprinted with permission; professional tip by Jo Verity, reprinted with permission of the author; haiku 'Water piccolos' by Adam Horovitz from THE SINGING BRINK: AN ANTHOLOGY OF POETRY FROM LUMB BANK edited by Maura Dooley and David Hunter, Arvon Press 1987 © Adam Horovitz, reprinted with kind permission of the author; haiku 'In the Lonely Valley' by Peter Mortimer, from THE SINGING BRINK: AN ANTHOLOGY OF POETRY FROM LUMB BANK edited by Maura Dooley and David Hunter, Arvon Press 1987 © Peter Mortimer, reprinted with kind permission of the author; 'How to Leave the World that Worships Should' by Ros Barber, from MATERIAL by Ros Barber, published by Anvil Press Poetry in 2008, reprinted

with permission of Anvil Press Poetry; 'This is Just to Say' by
William Carlos Williams, from COLLECTED POEMS published
by Carcanet Press, reprinted by permission of Carcanet Press
Limited; exercise by Jean Sprackland, reprinted with permission;
'Autumn' by Iain Crichton Smith, from COUNTRY FOR OLD
MEN AND MY CANADA published by Carcanet Press, reprinted
by permission of Carcanet Press Limited; 'The London Eye' by
Patience Agbabi, from BLOODSHOT MONOCHROME by
Patience Agbabi published by Bloodaxe Books, reprinted with
permission; 'Poem from a Bus Shelter' by Clare Shaw, from
STRAIGHT AHEAD published by Bloodaxe Books, reprinted
with permission of Bloodaxe Books; 'Heptonstall' by Ian Duhig,
from THE SINGING BRINK: AN ANTHOLOGY OF POETRY
FROM LUMB BANK edited by Maura Dooley and David Hunter,
Arvon Press 1987 © Ian Duhig, reprinted with kind permission
of the author; professional tip by Jacob Polley, reprinted with
permission; exercise adapted from one by Carol Angier and Sally
Cline, reprinted with permission; professional tip by Ian Marchant,
reprinted with permission; exercises by Miranda France, reprinted
with permission; professional tip by Christopher George,
reprinted with permission; professional tip by Caroline
Smailes, reprinted with permission; short extract from 'The
First Discovery' by Alfred Noyes from COLLECTED POEMS,
reprinted with permission of The Society of Authors as the
Literary Representative of the Estate of Alfred Noyes; professional
tip by Lee Weatherley, reprinted with permission; professional
tip by Jeremy Sheldon, reprinted with permission; short extract
from ON THE BLACK HILL by Bruce Chatwin, copyright ©
1982 by Bruce Chatwin. Used by permission of The Random
House Group Limited, UK and Viking Penguin, a division of
Penguin Group (USA) Inc; short extract from 'PARADISE' by
A. L. Kennedy, copyright © 2004 by A. L. Kennedy. Used by
permission of Alfred A. Knopf, a division of Random House, Inc
and Random House Group UK; exercises by Martyn Bedford,
reprinted with permission; short extract from NUNS AND
SOLDIERS by Iris Murdoch, published by Chatto & Windus,
reprinted with permission of The Random House Group Ltd
and Ed Victor Limited; professional tip by Monique Roffey,

reprinted with permission; short extract from AN UNSUITABLE
JOB FOR A WOMAN by P. D. James, reprinted with permission
of Greene & Heaton Ltd.; short extract from THE CEMENT
GARDENT by Ian McEwan, copyright © 1978 by Ian McEwan,
reprinted by permission of Random House Group UK and
Georges Borchardt Inc, on behalf of the author; professional tip
by Mavis Creek, reprinted with permission; professional tip by
Christopher Wakling, reprinted with permission; 3 lines from
'Drama Workshop' by Iain Crichton Smith, from COLLECTED
POEMS, published by Carcanet Press, reprinted with permission
of Carcanet Press Limited; professional tip by Willy Russell,
reprinted with permission; professional tip by Mark Illis, reprinted
with permission; professional tip by Jenny Lecoat, reprinted with
permission; professional tip by Camilla Hornby, reprinted with
permission.

The author and publisher also acknowledge the use of quotations
from:

'Ryokan, The Thief' haiku, from *The Enlightened Heart* by
Stephen Mitchell © 1989 by Stephen Mitchell, published by
HarperCollins, USA; 'In a Station of the Metro', haiku by Ezra
Pound, *Collected Poems*, Faber and Faber; 'Home is Sad' by Philip
Larkin, from THE WHITSUN WEDDINGS, Faber and Faber UK
and Farrar Straus & Giroux LLC USA; extract from *The Electric
Michelangelo* by Sarah Hall, published by Faber and Faber UK and
HarperCollins USA.

Contents

Meet the author

Welcome to *Get Started in Creative Writing*!

I'm guessing that the fact you are reading this book means you are now serious about your writing. I'm guessing too, that the fact you have taken the time to read this book rather than just leaping in to begin your novel or poetry collection means that you are not a brash type, over-burdened with self-belief and confidence. In fact, I imagine that the opposite is true. You already doubt yourself, wondering if you really have anything original to say or any way to properly express it. This self-doubt is one major reason you have put off doing anything with your writing until now. I know this. I've felt this too. We all have.

This feeling that you might not have any actual talent is one you share with nearly every writer, however successful they are. It's one of the things that marks you out as being a writer. Writers are quite horribly insecure: always unwilling to believe that they have written something worthwhile and at the same time touchy about criticism. Writing is a kind of emotional bungee jumping. We plunge into the depths and bounce back again higher than we thought possible, before falling to earth again. And, like bungee jumping, it's terrifying and exhilarating all at the same time.

But you have already taken an important step on the road to becoming the very best writer you can be. You have decided to enlist some help.

Some of your friends have probably tried to put you off reading a book like this (assuming that any of your friends know that you want to write – so many new writers keep it a secret, not wanting to be thought weird or that they are somehow 'getting above themselves'). 'You can't teach writing,' they say. 'Writers are born, not made.' And there is truth in that. The urge to write, and the determination to keep at it in spite of all the distractions that life puts in the way, has to be dredged from somewhere within you and no one can teach that. Though it gets easier with practice. The desire to improve is probably innate too. And you have already proved you have got that because you have bought or borrowed this book.

Get Started in Creative Writing is designed to save you time. It's a guide to the short cuts that you might miss if you were travelling what can be a lonely road entirely on your own.

But *Get Started in Creative Writing* is not a literary sat nav. It can't guide you to publication, fame and fortune in easy mechanically voiced steps. There's nothing contained within the pages of this book that you couldn't find out for yourself, but it might take you years of painful trial and error with many, many discouraging knock-backs along the way. You'll get some of those anyway – discouraging knock-backs are part of the process of becoming a fully realized human being, never mind becoming a writer – but this book will, I hope, mean that you skirt around the more obvious pitfalls, while honing a style that is uniquely yours.

What I have tried to do in *Get Started in Creative Writing* is to distil some of the best advice from writers who have between them spent many, many thousands of hours thinking about, talking about, and teaching writing.

I have drawn on the practical guidance of hundreds of writers in all genres and at all stages in their writing career. Some have given exercises which can be used to develop your skills and confidence. There are 100 practical exercises to generate ideas and professional tips from some of the best in the contemporary writing world. There are also various simple tests designed to test your fluency and confidence in any aspect of writing. And there is now support and help on the web too.

I have also, of course, drawn on my own background and practice as a struggling writer, as well as my time as a teacher. There are many exercises of my own which have sprung from my thinking about what might help a new writer who is unsure of the direction in which their writing may take them. And you can be sure that everything I have written is from the heart and tested by experience.

It is not necessary to do every exercise in order to benefit from this book. Nor is it necessary to do them in sequence. Equally, you might want to do those exercises that you personally find particularly useful several times. Some might become part of your daily practice. I hope so. In fact, though I use the word 'exercise' throughout, you might prefer to think of them as 'games' or ways into writing. Also, at the end of each chapter there are key facts, which you might find particularly useful to carry with you as you go through the course.

Writing is hard work, but it shouldn't feel like a slog. You should feel joy and pride too. The exercises here are workouts that will help you put on writing muscle, but they are fun too. I'd like to think that many of these exercises are suitable for more than the one genre. An exercise that works especially well for blossoming screenwriters, may also work for playwrights and novelists. Be creative and feel free to plot your own path through this book.

Get Started in Creative Writing is intended to give you a chance to attempt all the major forms of writing, and to provide you with the information you need to do this in an enjoyable way. Whether you decide that you are a poet, a short story writer, a novelist, a children's writer, a playwright, a screenwriter, a journalist, a blogger or any combination of these, then I hope this book will prove a useful and enjoyable companion. Whether you see writing as a hobby, as a way of passing on your memories or as a way of earning a living in the future, *Get Started in Creative Writing* should give you the building blocks you need. And I'm always interested in hearing from new writers, so feel free to get in touch via my website www.sdmay.com with your feedback or your own stories of your writing life.

The first edition of this book was written over ten years ago by the novelist and poet Dianne Doubtfire, and I'm indebted to her for her groundwork, just as I am to her former student, Ian Burton, who picked up the baton for subsequent editions. Some of their exercises remain. And of course I'd like to thank all the writers and students who helped provide material. Some did this directly, in the form of exercises, and others helped through informal conversations about writing, which were then transmuted into the substance of this book.

Good luck!

Stephen May

Only got a minute?

Forget what they say. Writing is easy. It is.

Unlike learning to play a musical instrument, writing does not demand hours and hours of repetitive practice every day. Neither does it demand expensive equipment. And unlike learning a foreign language you don't need to go abroad or find someone else to practise with.

All you need to write is a pen, some paper and a place to go. And it doesn't need to be a particularly quiet or private place. You can write on the tube, on the bus, in a café, during breaks at work, in bed. You can write during stolen moments at work, or after the kids have gone to bed. Writing in a car is perhaps not to be recommended, but even while driving there are ways of going about it. You can speak into a Dictaphone or MPS player. Or you can record your thoughts into a phone.

You don't need to be in perfect health or even physically fit. You don't have to have a degree or even a GCSE. You don't have to be young. You don't have to be good-looking. You don't have to be a certain age or a certain social class. Writing is completely democratic.

You just need to have something to say.

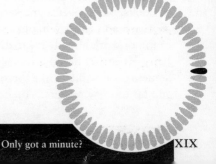

5 Only got five minutes?

Creative writing is easy, natural, healthy, sociable, cheap and accessible. Writing is easy because most people are educated enough to put thoughts down on paper. It is natural because to want to make sense of our lives and times is what makes us human. It is good for you because to seek to understand the world around us is to begin to change it. People who write live longer, more fulfilled lives than those who don't. This is because we are already turning our dreams into realities. Writing is sociable because writers gather in groups and classes in addition to working alone. Plus we collect stories from family members, workmates, passersby and people in pubs, cafés and churches. We can't help getting involved in the lives of others even if we work on the material we gather on our own.

The only reason not to write is if you simply want to get rich. You shouldn't write for the money because, generally speaking, there isn't any. Yes, I know that J. K. Rowling, John Grisham, Dan Brown and a hundred others have got rich through writing, but that isn't *why* they do it. The money is a bonus. They'd do it anyway. They write because they have something to say. In fact, more than this, they write because they have a compulsion. An itch that they have to scratch. You should write because, if you're a writer, you'll always be vaguely miserable (and a pain to be with) if you don't.

If that describes you, then you might as well just get on with it. But think hard about what it is you are trying to say. There are lots of books, plays, poems and scripts out there already. Why should anyone read yours? What have you got to say that adds to the huge canon of work already created?

Sometimes it will feel like there are too many writers in the world and far too few readers. You can feel like a beggar endlessly sleeve-tugging at disinterested passers-by. Writers are unique among artists because of their symbiotic relationship with individual readers. They must somehow entice readers to pick up their work and spend time with it alone, despite all the many competing pressures that might come from family, work, computer games or TV.

That can be hard. But if you work at your craft, and always remember that your stories have the same validity as anyone else's, then you will get noticed. And, although a writer needs readers, and these can be hard to find, you don't need very many. A few people genuinely looking forward to your next piece. That's enough. That's all you need.

Of course if you can't take criticism or rejection then writing isn't for you. All writers must face rejection; it's part of the job. It is much easier for editors and agents to say no, than to say yes and take a huge risk on something that may not work. After all, another writer will be along in less than a minute. So don't be offended by people saying no to you.

In fact, actually being ignored – being rejected – is good for your writing too. You have to learn to write smarter, to grab the attention and not let it go. You develop guile and flair and stamina and, as the lightweights drop out, you stand more chance of getting the audience you deserve.

Finally, find a voice that is uniquely yours. Stick to it. Grow with it. Tell the stories that only you can tell and eventually doors will open.

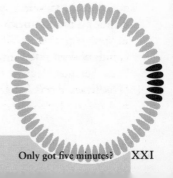

10 Only got ten minutes?

One question you will have to answer when beginning to write creatively is: what kind of work is this? Is my idea, or story, best expressed as a poem? As a novel? A memoir? A play? A TV or film script? Obviously at this stage you may well want to experiment with all kinds of writing but, while I firmly believe that good writing is good writing is good writing, there are particular rules to each genre. And knowing these might save you time.

Poetry

A poem is a tightly structured exploration of a single powerful idea or image. The poet will use a variety of musical and linguistic devices to investigate their story and make it visible for the reader. A poet may or may not use rhyme, but will certainly use a range of rhythmic devices to give the work impact. These devices may echo at an invisible level the theme of the poem. Much of what is happening in a poem should be taking place below the waterline of the words. The words simply show a way in for the readers who then find in the gaps and silences a meaning for themselves.

Modern poetry is perhaps the most ignored of all the arts and yet it thrives in a vigorous sub-culture of readings, competitions, small magazines and on the net, and is promoted by a number of energetic independent publishers. Mainstream publishers like Faber and Faber and Jonathan Cape continue to support poetry, though not with the vigour of past decades. This is largely because it makes no money: neither for the poets nor for the publishers.

Good modern poets include Neil Rollinson, Ros Barber, Sharon Olds, Seamus Heaney, Simon Armitage, Carol Ann Duffy, Leanne O'Sullivan, Fiona Sampson, John Burnside, Kathleen Jamie,

Jen Hadfield, Jacob Polley, Penelope Shuttle, Graham Mort, Kate Bingham, Fleur Adcock, Alan Brownjohn, Elizabeth Alexander, Clare Pollard and Selima Hill.

Novels

Unlike poetry, novels have not been with us that long in historical terms. Daniel Defoe was one of the first novelists, and with his work *Moll Flanders* (1722) he seemed to establish the template for all future novels. *Moll Flanders* is the tale of the eponymous heroine's journey from desperate beginnings to a life of virtue, via spells as a prostitute, a thief and a con-artist. Along the way most of those who have contact with Moll either abuse her, or are abused by her. This early novel is entirely modern in mixing a page-turning plot with insights into the foibles of contemporary life. Defoe doubtless drew on his own incredibly varied life experiences, but was also using his considerable powers of invention. A novel is not the simple retelling of the author's life.

Whether a novel is a literary work (essentially a book that seeks to entertain and enrich through its use of language as well as by its story), or a more straightforward genre novel (crime, thriller, romance, chick-lit, historical drama), it will be driven by strong characters in conflict with one another, or with the life they are forced to lead. A novel – of whatever type – will be propelled by its story. Characters, however richly imagined, will need to actually *do* things for your readers to stay interested. It seems obvious but it's actually far harder to pull off than you might think.

For good, ambitious, modern novelists try Jill Dawson, Tobias Hill, John Banville, Deborah Levy, Christopher George, Monique Roffey, Sarah Hall, Zadie Smith, Marcel Theroux, Cormac McCarthy, Nick Hornby, Mavis Cheek, Martin Amis, Alan Warner and Suzanne Berne.

Plays

Writers often make the mistake of thinking plays are about speeches. They are not. They are not even about words really. The dialogue in a play exists to give actors something to do, rather than something to say. Plays are about characters forced to act because of pressures from their own nature, or because of outside events.

A common fault of new playwrights is to over-write and to write on-the-nose or obvious dialogue. Drama is real life distilled to its essence and in real life, people rarely say what it is they really want for fear of ridicule or rejection. Increasingly too, modern playwrights and directors will want to explore the physicality of a drama, expressing action through inventive non-realistic physical action.

If you are interested in writing drama then make sure you see as much new work as you can. Your local theatre will probably have a few weeks set aside to promote new writing. Make the effort to get there and see what's going on. And check out the work of newer writers such as Rebecca Lenkiewicz, Rona Munro, Roy Williams, Simon Stephens, Enda Walsh and Gregory Burke.

Screenwriting

All writing is a collaboration. Even if you are writing poetry there are editors suggesting changes. With film and television writing, the eventual product is the result of many minds working on a piece separately or together over many months or even years. All writing is rewriting too. Novels and autobiographies will go through several drafts supervised by agents and editors as well as authors, but in film and television this process is hugely elongated. Many, many hands will make their mark on a script before it is finally screened. The writer is far from being the most important figure in this process. The producer and director may well have much more clout. And with film and television production companies taking such huge financial risks, then the money people will also want their say.

The rules for film and television genres are more firmly fixed too. Screenwriting has become endangered as audiences desert TVs and cinemas for the pleasures of shopping and chatting to each other on the internet. And in a world where every programme and every film ever made is available more or less instantly via the PC, it is hard for new ideas to make an impact. However, there are also more outlets for work than ever before, so there are still opportunities for good new screenwriters.

Life-writing

A biography or memoir may be about real life, but it still requires creative writing skills. You may not want to put raw fiction into your piece but the process of selection and editing of facts, as well as the slippery business of memory itself, will mean your work will hardly be the definitive truth of a life. In any case you have the same duty to your readers to provide all the complex entertainment that any other form of writing does. Your audience deserve engaging stories, fully developed characters, absorbing prose and striking imagery. It can't be any less worked on just because it's the truth.

Whichever path you choose, if you are serious about writing then it is only right that you do your homework. Read other people's work, especially that by new writers, and look outside the mainstream for exciting new talents. Check out who is being talked about on literary blogs and who is being published by the smaller publishers. Writing is about widening the horizons of the whole culture, so make sure yours are as broad as possible.

1

Why write?

In this chapter you will learn:
- *some motivations for writing*
- *how writing helps make sense of living*
- *how to begin*
- *what you will need.*

Why did I write? Because I found life unsatisfactory.

Tennessee Williams

Writing is easy

More or less every adult in this country can write. Despite what we read and hear, teachers are not doing so bad a job that many pupils leave school illiterate. Most of us can fashion a sentence, however clumsily. In addition, many people who would never consider themselves to be writers can use words very well. Think of the people you know at work, or among your friends and family, who are natural storytellers – people who can hold a group enthralled with a vivid account of something that happened to them, or who can get a room to explode in laughter with a quick one-liner. There is every likelihood that you know many people who are famed among their peers for their skill with words, and not one of them would consider themselves to be a writer. There are people whose emails or texts are a joy to read because they have a special colour with which they use language, even if it is dealing with something really quite dull.

The famous Czech writer Franz Kafka had a day-job as an insurance clerk but by all accounts, his reports and minutes were eagerly awaited by his colleagues because of their dry humour and elegant phrasing.

Insight

Maybe you are one of these people too. Maybe you are someone who enjoys telling stories, or who gets a buzz from putting words in the right order; someone who delights in entertaining, informing and surprising friends, family and colleagues with words.

Exercise 1

Write down in one sentence (no more than 30 words) why it is that you want to write.

Writing is natural

The philosopher Socrates said 'The unexamined life is not worth living' and *his* words, as transcribed by Plato, have survived for several thousand years, so he knew what he was talking about. We live busy lives at a frantic pace. There often doesn't seem time just to 'stand and stare' as the poet W. H. Davies put it.

We spend so much of our time firefighting – reacting to events – that we leave ourselves little time to investigate the causes of all the small blazes in our lives. Why do we do the things we do? Why do we often feel hurt, neglected or sad? How can we be better parents, children, companions or lovers? How can we make sense of a world that contains 6 billion people? What is the point of it all?

Insight

Surely at least part of the point of life is to decide who we are and then to try and become that person? And how can we do that if we don't try and express our own unique way of seeing the world?

For some people their natural mode of self-expression will be one of the other arts. They will form a band, or join a choir. They might take photographs or paint. Others will want to act or make films or create conceptual art. Still others will find that the extraordinary advances in digital technology will lead them down pathways to self-expression that didn't even exist ten years ago. But more and more of us, even in a digital world, want to use one of the oldest and simplest forms of self-expression. We want to tell stories. We want to tell our own stories or make up new ones. We want to transform our own existence into words that will delight, entertain, amuse or even horrify others.

The great English poet Ted Hughes believed that all these words had value. He believed that they all added to the 'sacred book of the tribe'. Our individual attempts to make sense of our lives contribute to the way humanity itself discovers its nature and purpose. In this sense at least, everyone's story has equal value.

The beauty of the written word, as opposed to the spoken word in film and television, is that it invites you to linger. Film and television writing moves on at an ever faster pace, as the techniques and technology of editing develop. But a book or a poem allows the reader to choose the pace at which a story unfolds. We can immediately revisit passages that we especially like, take our time to unravel anything that we find obscure or difficult. But plays, films and television have their place in making sense of the world and we'll cover those art forms too, later in this book.

Creative writing is good for you

Writing is a good way to reduce stress and relieve depression. Simply writing troubles down makes them seem more manageable. Reliving past traumas on the page can reduce their power to haunt. Writing is a way of taking control over your life. Therapy might not be your primary motivation for becoming a writer, but writing is certainly an effective way of keeping anxiety at bay. In fact, I can say that if you write regularly you will look and feel better without even needing to get up from your chair! It is that powerful a magic.

CREATIVE WRITING IS SOCIABLE

This might seem an odd thing to say: the usual image of a writer is someone who is solitary, a hermit. And it is true that in order to write successfully you need to have the ability and the discipline to shut yourself off in a room on your own. But writers also form a community and as we begin to take our work more seriously, the more important that community will be to us.

Of course a lot of writers work with others anyway. Film and television writers are working with a whole army of collaborators from the director to the stylist, from the producer to the gaffer's grip-boy (whatever that is)!

Playwrights work even more closely with the directors and actors. But even for poets and novelists the need for peer support can be incredibly important. As you become more confident with your writing you will probably want to join a local group of fellow writers. You will want to find supportive but candid friends who can act as first readers and trusted guides. You will also find personal benefits in providing this service for other people. You might want to attend intensive residential courses like those run by the Arvon Foundation. You might even end up deciding to undertake an MA in Creative Writing. But whatever paths writing leads you down you are bound to end up meeting like-minded people who are stimulating – sometimes infuriating – to be around. I'll write at greater length about the writing community in Chapter 20, 'Moving on'.

CREATIVE WRITING IS CHEAP AND ACCESSIBLE

If you want to be a top sports pro it is unlikely that you are going to be able to get one-to-one tuition from the very best players and coaches. Even if you could afford it, how would you persuade someone like Andy Murray to give you a series of private lessons? He's a busy man! And the same is true of many other arts too. But in the field of creative writing your perfect mentors are always around, always available. If you use your public library then your favourite authors are there, they are free, and they are present for as long as you need them. There is absolutely nothing to stop you spending weeks locked up alone with Tolstoy, or with Philip Roth, Sharon Olds, Sylvia Plath, Jackie Collins or Woody Allen.

Insight

Whoever your inspiration is then they are waiting for you. Dead or alive, mad or bad, the greatest writers are available as your guides. You don't have to rely on YouTube or on grainy footage of long-lost champions in order to study technique; you can bring their work home with you and focus on it in microscopic detail in your own home and in your own time. How-To books like this one are useful but by no means essential.

Exercise 3

Make a short list of the writers whose works you have found most inspiring. Now make sure that you fit in a trip to the public library when you next go shopping and take out some of their work. Reacquaint yourself with your heroes.

Exercise 4

This is about trying to find some new heroes. Ask around among your friends, family and work colleagues for examples of writing that they have found particularly impressive. When you return your heroes to the library, make sure you replace them with some writing that has been recommended to you. Reading, more than anything else, is what will help you to improve as a writer. Reading good work carefully is the fastest way to see visible developments in your own writing life. And it helps to have an open mind and a willingness to experiment in your reading tastes too. Try not to be too dismissive of work you see being championed in the press or on television. On the other hand, reading something and then thinking, 'I could do better than that' is a perfectly legitimate response. It can be very inspiring to find some writer who has legions of admirers but who you think is not actually such hot stuff. That's fine. I'd keep it to yourself for a little while, however!

CREATIVE WRITING IS A FAMILY AFFAIR

Writing creatively is a good way to get and stay close to your family. Older family members may well have interesting stories and family secrets that can act as springboards for your own work. Your children and other younger relatives may want to know about the stories that you can tell. Very young children, of course, love stories, whether real or imagined, and are a very good and truthful audience.

Insight

If you are open about your writing you might quickly find that it grows into a family project with people regularly asking you for bulletins as to how the work is progressing. This can be a good motivation for carrying on with it.

Exercise 5

Ask someone in your extended family for a story that they haven't told you before. They don't have to be convinced that it is entirely true, it could be some kind of family legend from the distant past. Take notes and put them in a drawer to be worked on later.

Finding time to write

Everyone has time to write. It might be that something else will have to go (a favourite television show, staying late at the office, looking for eBay bargains, reading the paper – writers make sacrifices, there's no getting around this), but you'll find the time to write if you want to badly enough. Suzanne Berne, the Orange prize-winning author of *A Crime in the Neighborhood*, wrote her first book having been determined to set aside at least five minutes a day in which to write. If she achieved at least her daily five minutes then she gave herself a little tick on her calendar. 'After a little while,' she says, 'I became obsessed with giving myself a tick every day. And if you can somehow manage a page a day, that's a novel in a year.'

> **Insight**
> If you write 1,000 words a day, that works out at a novel twice the length of *Great Expectations* every single year.

The double Carnegie medal-winning children's author Berlie Doherty put a log on the fire after her children went to bed and wrote until the log burnt out. Serious writers, those who make a success of it, will make time.

However much or little you write, regularity is the most important thing. Suzanne Berne's five minutes a day will achieve better results than a four-hour stretch every now and again. If you are really struggling to find time then try managing on seven hours' sleep instead of eight. If this doesn't work, then you have no choice: you have to get rid of the television. Nothing steals so much time, nor does it in so insidious a manner, as the television. You'll also save the cost of the licence fee in the UK and any digital or cable subscriptions too. Which means that writing will already be paying off for you.

THE SECOND-BEST TIME

There's a saying: 'The best time to plant a tree is 20 years ago. The second-best time is now.' Of course you should really have got down to writing before this. But you can't do anything about that. Don't fret. Let it go.

Writing is one of those things that you can begin at any age. I've already mentioned that it doesn't require physical fitness, youth or even good health. Don't worry that some publishers seem to be like pop impresarios these days, always looking for a moody-looking teenager with a wild haircut and astonishing cheekbones; that some of them seem to regard their job as a branch of showbiz. We know otherwise and so do readers.

You have got to have lived a bit, and looked and listened a lot, before you have enough to say. Everything that has happened to you up to now is your material. The older you are the more material you have to draw on. You are in a better position than someone just out of college. Wordsworth described writing as 'experience recollected in tranquillity'. And so the more experience you have the better. You just need to make sure that you can find those moments of tranquillity!

A word about technology

You don't need a laptop to be a writer. And having one doesn't make you a writer either.

A light, simple-to-use laptop might be very useful, but it is by no means essential. The great Californian crime writer Peter Plate once found himself facing students upset that a temporary power failure meant that the computers weren't working in the building where he was conducting a writing class. His calm response made a powerful impression on me. He said, 'Don't confuse convenience with utility'. And with that he sent everyone off to write with a pencil.

Fewer people were interested in writing years ago and at least part of the reason was because it took a lot more physical effort to write using longhand or a typewriter. Writing was physical labour; words were almost literally wrenched from the writer. At any rate writers were very much connected to their words in a physical way.

Insight
Work on a PC looks deceptively finished at an early stage. Cut and paste facilities can trick you into believing that you are carrying out a serious edit when in fact you are merely moving inadequate material from one place to another.

Now, I'm not so much of a Luddite as to suggest that new writers should get rid of their PCs – for one thing the internet can be an important market for a writer as well as a valuable research tool – but we should all be aware that just because our work looks professionally solid in its beautiful font, it doesn't mean that the writing itself is any good. The comfort that modern technology brings means that we have to be strict with ourselves.

The next chapter explores how to find ideas and inspiration that will unlock your authentic voice and so begin to create the writing that is distinctively yours, but before that here is a simple exercise that helps you realize just how subtle great writing can be.

Exercise 6

Go to a book you love. Open it at random and copy out a paragraph. That's it. (Poets will want to copy out a poem.) Repeat this process two or three times with different books. It will give you a physical sense of how that writing was built up. Teachers of other art forms, such as music or painting, are very keen on getting practitioners to copy before they move on to original modes of expression. For obvious reasons writers haven't intentionally copied other people's work since the invention of the printing press. But a small taste of it in this way can be quite helpful in bringing you close to the rhythm and pulse of your favourite writers. It's a way of giving you a physical sense of how they go about building effective passages of writing.

Professional tip from John Siddique

I became a writer after reading the E. E. Cummings poem 'Somewhere I Have Never Travelled'. That poem reflected a world inside me and made me want to do the same for others. It made me realize you could write about small things, ordinary things and still have a big effect. I put some of this into my poem 'To Writing'.

To Writing

*Until you came I had no voice of my own, I would
borrow song lyrics for my feelings, use films as examples.
Struggle for words. Always. Always.
Before you came, I was an illiterate marking an x instead
of saying my name. Face down in shame. Always outcast.
I throw myself into you, an unrequited
lover, expecting all the rewards I had dreamed, maybe
even a taste of the unnameable things, but you
are not love, though you are my one and only.
Showing me treasure. Feeding me with so many stories.
When the poem is over, the audience leaves it's just
you and me again.*

From *The Prize* (Rialto)

John Siddique is a poet and teacher.

10 THINGS TO REMEMBER

1 *Let everyone know you are writing. It will help you keep focused.*

2 *Make time to write every day, even if it's only for a few minutes.*

3 *Use the library to reacquaint yourself with writers you love.*

4 *Experiment by reading new writers.*

5 *Read reviews, see what's out there.*

6 *Don't worry about all the time that's past –.it's what you write now and in the future that counts.*

7 *Copy out a piece of writing you love.*

8 *Don't worry about buying expensive laptops or PCs. A pen and a cheap notepad will do.*

9 *Join a writing group if you can.*

10 *Don't write for money. There isn't any.*

2

Ideas and inspirations

In this chapter you will learn:
- *how to generate ideas*
- *how to develop ideas*
- *the potential of your ideas.*

> *Inspiration does exist... but it has to find you working.*
>
> Pablo Picasso

Capturing ideas

Your notebook is a weapon for holding those free-range thoughts.

Ideas are tricky little creatures. There are always millions around. More than enough for all the writers that have ever been, or ever will be. One sort are the organic, free-range ideas that run through your head at all sorts of odd times. These can be speedy, fleeting, even ghostly creatures that are hard to catch. But if you make sure that you have a notebook to hand at all times then you will stand a good chance of corralling them and developing them, so that these stray, wild creatures become fully formed and wholly yours.

Sometimes you will pin these ideas into the pages of your book and, on returning to them, find that they have withered away. Sometimes they were so spindly that they had no chance of growing to a usable size however much you fed or watered them.

It's perhaps best to think of ideas, elusive and slippery things that they are, not as thoughts but as *opportunities*. All of them may grow into the thing that helps you produce a great piece of work: something that may even make your name and your reputation. If you don't catch them as they pass, they will disappear. Don't trust that you will remember them or recapture the essence later, you almost certainly won't. If you don't write them down they will vanish, leaving just a sulphuric whiff of frustration and lost opportunity.

Even worse than this, someone else may catch hold of a similar idea (it won't be exactly the same, it may not even be as good) and you will find yourself confronted with the opportunity that became someone else's reputation-cementing piece of work.

Always, always, always, always have a notebook on hand. You may well find that, as your writing life develops, you become something of a stationery addict, haunting suppliers in search of notebooks of the perfect size or a make of pen that won't let you down. And it's right that you become obsessive about pens and notebooks; it's right that you fret and worry about paper thickness and the quality of spines and binding. These are the weapons of the idea hunter. Just as an angler checks that his rods and his wheels and his lines are up to the task of wrestling his prize to the net, so you should ensure that your tools are the kind that will help you make sure no idea ever escapes you.

Generating your own ideas

Some useful ideas may hurtle out of the sky, or scurry through your mind as if from nowhere. Others you may have to nurture from scratch. Either way, the blank page is always a tyrant to any writer, which is why so many start the day with automatic or free writing. Anything to stop the oppression of all that white space.

Exercise 7

Try your hand at free writing. Set an alarm clock, cell phone or kitchen timer to go off after five minutes and just keep writing for the whole of that time. Don't allow your conscious mind to interfere, just keep writing. Keep your pen moving for the whole period. At least one useful nugget will emerge that might be worked on later. More than this, however, the act of writing, under pressure but without an editor or critic in your head, will help loosen you up for the challenges of your current writing project.

Insight

Many, many writers are fervent believers in the idea of morning pages: of getting up and writing first thing, before you have had a coffee, showered or washed your face. This, they believe, is when you are most in touch with your subconscious self and able to tap into the rich seams of material that gets buried during the working day.

Many writers conscientiously keep dream diaries as repositories of the strange wisdom that comes to us all in the night, and which we can draw on later when creating our polished work.

Using what only you know

There are exercises that can help force ideas to the surface the way that beaters are employed to force game birds into the sky for the hunters to bag.

Exercise 8

Writing what you know is probably the single most common piece of advice handed out to a new writer. And it clearly makes sense, as this exercise shows.

1 *Draw up a list of all the jobs you have had.*
2 *Now write down all the places you have been to in the last five years.*
3 *Write down all the places you have ever lived.*
4 *Add to this list all the people whom you have worked with.*
5 *Write down your hobbies and interests.*
6 *Write down the names, jobs or interests of all the people you know best.*

You should by now have pages and pages of possible material. Suddenly there in front of you are tremendous possibilities for exciting writing that no one else can produce. No one else has quite this collection of characters, settings, stories or experiences. This exercise is a great one for making concrete the sheer wealth of material you have at your fingertips.

There has been an enormous explosion in the number of people researching and writing about their family history. When the 1901 census for England and Wales was first put online in 2002, it received 50 million hits on the first day and crashed. But lists of names and dates and occupations are one thing; what about the real life, the living breathing human beings, behind these connections?

Exercise 9

Choose someone from your own family tree and try to imagine how you might convey their unique personality to someone who has never met them. Start with the obvious and work inwards. Where was she born? Where did she live? What work did she do? But try to move quickly on to the things that make this person real. How did she dress? How did she speak? What made her laugh? What made her sad? Did she have favourite sayings? Any particular mannerisms? Any interesting quirks or habits? Try to get all this down in 300 words. Remember that at this stage we are not counting every word, but we are making every word count.

Here is a simple exercise that I first saw used in a workshop by the poets Colette Bryce and Matthew Hollis and it's great for making you think about your parents in a new light.

Exercise 10

Try to imagine your parents together before you were born. Try and place them in a specific situation, doing something together. Are they on honeymoon? On holiday? Or visiting friends? Are they quietly sitting side-by-side in the evening or are they arguing passionately, fiercely about something? Is there harmony in this situation or conflict? Are they in a town or a house you know well, or somewhere where you have never been? Do they have brothers or sisters on the scene or are they alone? Or are they with their parents perhaps?

See if you can write just 100 or 200 words on this.

INCLUDING WHAT YOU DON'T KNOW

Here is an exercise that stresses the importance of making every word count and it's one I learned from the novelist, short story writer and screenwriter Mark Illis. It's great as an ice-breaker but it also builds on what has gone before and introduces one key new element. This time you are not only writing about what you know best – yourself – but you are also writing what you *don't* know. This is every bit as much of a writer's job as drawing on your own experience. Making stuff up is part of the job description.

Exercise 11

Your task is to write your autobiography in exactly 50 words. Not 49. Not 51. Exactly 50. And it must also contain one lie. As an example, here is one that I did...

Stephen May was a sickly child. Born in Norfolk, schooled in Bedford but with Scottish parents. He has been a barman, a journalist, a warehouseman, a teacher and a model. He was also thrown out of his teenage punk band after being seen dancing to Abba records at a party.

Naturally, I'm not going to tell you what my lie is...

Using magazines and newspapers

These can be great inspirations for your own writing. Usually the headline stories won't be the things that capture your imagination. It can be the smaller snippets that lead you to think 'What if...', which leads on to, 'Let's pretend...'. The poet Amanda Dalton kept an article for years about a woman who abandoned her house to live in the garden, building a kind of nest out there from leaves and twigs and bits of rubbish. Her fascination with this woman and the possible reasons for her leading this life grew at last into the sequence of poems called 'Room of Leaves' in her first collection (*How To Disappear* – published by Bloodaxe) and then into an acclaimed radio play. The initial story was just a few lines long but it planted itself in her imagination, growing to fruition over months and years.

Exercise 12

Look through today's newspapers. Is there a story there that intrigues you, that excites your curiosity? Something where you want to know more about the characters than the writer is telling you? Cut it out and save it to work on later. Or maybe paste it into your notebook.

Now use the internet to have a look at a local paper from a foreign country. If you can read another language fluently so much the better, but this exercise works just as well if you look at newspapers from Australia, Canada, the USA, or another English-speaking country. Find a story that seems strange to you and read it carefully. Now imagine this same kind of story happening in the streets of your own town. What would stay the same, what would change? What kind of characters might become involved? For example, a story about a driver hitting a moose in the Canadian wilderness is obviously going to change dramatically if that moose was hit in Chipping Norton or East Grinstead.

MAKING THE UNLIKELY A REALITY

Another simple way to get the imagination working is to put yourself in an unlikely situation and to imagine how you might cope. Here is an exercise that was given to me by the short story writer and novelist Lynne Bryan. The original idea for this exercise came from a tiny story in Lynne's local paper.

Exercise 13

Imagine that two people are trapped overnight in a safe. It's a large safe but nevertheless a small, cramped, stifling place for two people. Your task is to decide:

▶ *who these two people are*
▶ *how they came to be in the safe*
▶ *what their relationship is to one another*
▶ *what it is like to spend the night in the safe*
▶ *what their emotions are upon being rescued in the morning.*

Very few people have been trapped in a safe, but all of us can imagine the emotions and sensations this kind of situation could create: boredom, anger, despair, acute anxiety, to name just four.

An extension of the exercise above can be to imagine two figures from history together in this situation or one like it. One writer friend I know is working on a very funny play where the poet Philip Larkin and the filmmaker Quentin Tarantino are stuck together, tied up in a video shop after a heist.

Another variant on this exercise might be to draw up two columns, one containing a list of modern celebrities and another a list of historical figures. Pick one from each list and imagine a meeting in extreme conditions and what might happen.

The essential thing is to be receptive to all the ideas that are out there. For a writer everything is material to be processed, transformed, celebrated or examined. Be open to taking inspiration from anywhere, however unlikely a source. There are millions of stories, poems, plays, films and articles in circulation already, but none of them say what only you can say in the way that only you can say it.

Once you start to wander through the world – preferably with your notebook in your hand – looking at the world through writer's eyes, you will see that almost everything can be mined for material. Don't worry too much at this stage about being original. It's far, far better to be good.

Professional tip from David Armstrong

There are only a certain number of ideas in the world. The good news is that no one knows just how many that number is; the bad news is that people have been mining the seam for a very long time. To write a story, perhaps a novel, what you have to do is conjure a new variation on one of the ideas that has been around for hundreds, if not thousands of years already.

Take comfort: it's said that Shakespeare didn't have an original idea for any of his plays, but whether he turned to the Romans, the Greeks or English historians, he took that source material and with it he spun pure gold.

David Armstrong is a successful writer of crime novels, including *Night's Black Angel* (HarperCollins).

10 THINGS TO REMEMBER

1 *Begin each writing session – however short – with some time free writing.*

2 *Always have a notebook to hand.*

3 *Any idea is worth recording – you don't know when it will be useful.*

4 *Cut out – or bookmark – stories that grab your attention in newspapers, magazines or on the web.*

5 *Carry a digital camera with you.*

6 *Look out for portraits and inspirational pictures in museums and galleries.*

7 *Write down interesting anecdotes or stories that have been in your family for years.*

8 *Put contrasting personalities in close proximity without means of escape.*

9 *It's easier to be original than good. But good is better.*

10 *Do more listening than you do talking. Your old granddad was right when he said there was a reason that we were given two ears and only one mouth. If you are telling a story you can't be getting someone else's.*

3

The feature article

In this chapter you will learn:
- *how to choose a subject for an article*
- *how to identify a market*
- *how to approach an editor.*

  Give someone half a page in a newspaper and they think
  they own the world.

Jeffrey Bernard

What is an article?

An article is not an essay, although it might sometimes resemble
one. An article is not a fictional piece, although it may contain
anecdotes or stories that are only half-true, or which build on
the truth in the interest of entertaining a reader. An article is not
usually a straightforward opinion piece, although again, it might
be. It really depends on whom your article is aimed at and, as
there are over 650 specialist magazines in the UK, what constitutes
an article might vary considerably. But in case this sounds too
daunting, consider the upside: 650 specialist magazines means 650
editors looking to fill a lot of pages every month or every week.
It also means that there is a lot of competition between editors
for the best material. Sure, they have staff writers to produce
regular pieces, but a lot of papers and magazines take work from
freelancers and it can be a rewarding way for new writers to learn
their craft and earn some income.

This is covered in more detail in *Get Your Articles Published* by Lesley Bown and Ann Gawthorpe.

Choosing a subject

Successful articles usually fall under one of these headings:

SPECIALIZED KNOWLEDGE

A subject where the writer has a thorough knowledge. For example, Beekeeping, Budapest, Poland, Home education, Vegan cookery, Computer gaming, Women's rugby – the list is literally endless and everyone is an expert in something.

AN UNUSUAL ANGLE

This involves taking an everyday subject and applying a fresh angle to it. For example, an article about family meals might be too ordinary, but the difficulties of planning them around World Cup viewing might be interesting.

HUMOUR

If you can write a genuinely funny piece, then you will find that anything can be your subject.

Insight

Write funny pieces regularly and you will find editors beginning to helicopter money over to you. Being funny is incredibly difficult but if you can crack it in the world of newspapers and magazines you might well never need to do a proper job ever again. It really is that rare a talent.

TOPICALITY

Magazine editing is a little like farming: there are definite seasons where stories, like a farmer's crops, have to be planted. There will always be Christmas articles, Halloween articles, summer holiday articles and so on. Also anniversaries need commemorating. The centenary of the birth of a famous (or infamous) person. A decade since a major event and so on. Remember to allow yourself enough time to plan. This book is being written in 2009 and will appear in 2010. 2010 means 40 years since the student uprisings in Paris. It means 50 years since John F. Kennedy became president of the USA. 50 years since the first man in space. 50 years since The Beatles first went to Hamburg and 40 years since they officially broke up. It means 25 years since Live Aid and 100 years since the first Urdu language typewriter was produced. These are all events which I can guarantee will be extensively revisited by magazines. (Well, possibly not the invention of the Urdu typewriter, at least not in the inward-looking West.)

As a writer of features reading this in 2010 you should really be wondering what anniversaries are coming up in 2011 (100 years since British MPs first voted to give themselves salaries; 100 years since the first airmail service was launched; 10 years since the twin towers of the World Trade Center were destroyed in the 9/11 attack). Furthermore, if you are reading this in spring then you should be planning articles that fit autumn and winter.

REAL LIFE

In the last few years there has been a huge expansion in the market for 'real life' stories. Whole magazines are dedicated to finding and telling the extraordinary true stories of ordinary people. And everyone has these stories. You do. And even if you don't then your friends and family do. Ask around. Encourage people to talk to you. Editors are desperate to find the most engaging human stories out there and will pay accordingly.

UNREAL LIFE

These are the stories about celebrity culture. Often the magazines that are interested in the extraordinary goings-on in the lives of ordinary people are also the same publications interested in the banal minutiae of celebrity life. And if you can get hold of an extraordinary story about, or interview with, anyone who is regularly in the public eye, then you will find a ready market for that too. And they don't have to be top film stars or sports people or music stars either. Television presenters, soap actors, weather girls and internet entrepreneurs can all be worthy of a story. On rare occasions, writers can be fair game too. Obviously, don't stalk anyone. Go through the proper channels. A courteous letter or email to an agent might have surprising and positive results.

MARKET STUDY

An obvious thing to say is that you should study very closely the magazines which you wish to write for. The author of the first edition of this book, Dianne Doubtfire, tells a story of a writer she knew who once sent an article on karate to a magazine for genteel ladies. 'They should all learn how to defend themselves', he said. The piece was not commissioned.

The magazines you choose for your market study will be the ones that you enjoy reading, the ones that specialize in your own particular interests.

Exercise 14

Before writing your article, do the following:

1 *Choose a subject area.*
2 *Choose several magazines that cover this subject.*
3 *Study the length of sample articles in the magazines. Nothing can really beat counting the actual words in a piece, however tedious this sounds. If you get the length wrong, then it doesn't matter how brilliant the feature, it won't be used.*
4 *Look at the style and content of the articles in several recent issues (editors change with almost alarming frequency and with them editorial policies). Take particular note of the page layout – the way the feature looks on the page.*

5 *How many photos are used?*
6 *Are text or fact boxes, or sidebars, used to provide the reader with additional information outside of the main text? These could be the listing of useful addresses, sources of further information, etc. If this is the case then you should take this into account when writing your own piece. This will demonstrate to an editor that you are familiar with the style of the magazine.*
7 *You should now have lots of notes on each title. Make sure you keep them separate for future reference.*

Your first article – a step-by-step guide

If you follow the steps outlined below then you should have an interesting piece of writing that will at least intrigue an editor. I would then read on to the end of the chapter and go back and correct and redraft in the light of the other notes and suggestions that I will give you. And then send it off if you are convinced that it is the best you can do. However, you must realize that you will almost certainly get a rejection the first few times that you do this. You may not even receive an acknowledgement for weeks or months. This is normal and you mustn't take it personally. Rejection is part of a writer's life. Developing a thick skin is a necessary part of learning the craft. It might help to think of the end result of all these exercises as being able to gather rejection slips, rather than achieving publication. Each slip then becomes a kind of certificate that shows that you are putting in the work, laying the foundations. This then becomes a reward in itself.

1 **Choose your subject**, *making sure that it falls under the heading of 'Specialized knowledge', 'Unusual angle', 'Humour', 'Topicality' or 'Real\unreal life'.*
2 **Select a possible market** *before you begin. Professional writers usually decide on a market beforehand and, even though you*

are an unpractised writer, having a goal in mind will act as a powerful incentive to produce your best work.

3   **Think** *about all the points you want to make in your article and jot them down in any order, just as they come to you.*

4   **Sort** *through these points, keeping the best but jettisoning any that seem irrelevant or repeat those you've already got down.*

5   **Plan** *the order of your points, bearing in mind that it is the opening which must have the most impact. Articles often have a reverse order to other kinds of writing in that the climax comes first. Your reader must be hooked enough to keep reading.*

6   **Write the first draft** *and don't worry about style at this point. Just get it down in the order that you have planned. Once you've got it on the page you will see how best to cut it, and where to get rid of any wasted or unnecessary words.*

7   **Choose a short snappy title.**

8   **Double-check all your facts** *and make sure that they are up to date. Editors rely on their contributors to know what they are writing about. If you get something wrong you will struggle to place work with that editor again.*

9   **Put your article in a drawer and wait.** *While your article is out of view a miraculous thing will happen. Your subconscious will work on it and when you retrieve it you will see more mistakes and more clunking prose and more excess verbiage than you thought possible. If you don't want to twiddle your thumbs during this vital stage, then begin another article or another piece of writing.*

10 **Write a second draft.** *Rewriting and editing are the hardest, least enjoyable tasks in writing – and probably the most necessary. But if you have waited while your piece ferments out of your sight for a week, then you may find that this important stage is much easier and more enjoyable than you thought it would be. Cutting can be as creative as writing if it is done with brio and courage.*

11 **Get some feedback.** *If you belong to a writers' group (and you probably should), now is the time to submit your piece to them. Or get your more candid friends to read it. You won't agree with everything said, but you will get at least one piece*

of helpful advice and you'll be needing a fresh perspective after spending so much time on revision.

12 **Send a query letter** *to the features editor. This letter should be brief and informative, outlining the subject matter, the length, the pictures that you would provide and so on. If you have specialist knowledge of the subject then you should say so here. If you do receive a positive response then you will be able to send out your article by return post (or, increasingly, by email) knowing it is going to an interested editor rather than going on to a slush pile where it will wait its turn along with many others, before being given a cursory glance by the work-experience kid.*

13 **Sending your work out.** *When you feel that your article is ready for submission, type it in double spacing on A4 paper (assuming that an interested editor hasn't asked for it to be sent as an attachment to an email). Pay attention to detail; editors are busy, professional people and they like their contributors to take similar pains. Some writers are given a lot of leeway. The columnist A. A. Gill is dyslexic and his manuscripts are littered with spelling mistakes of an original, almost indecipherable nature. Don't assume that an editor will look past an untidy manuscript to the gold that lies beneath. He probably won't. He doesn't have time. A. A. Gill gets away with it because, well, he is A. A. Gill and has a track record as a wit and critic. You don't. Yet.*

14 **Topical features.** *Be sure to submit a topical article in good time: two to three months ahead for a weekly magazine; four to six months for a monthly. Many editors buy their Christmas articles in June or earlier.*

Approaching an editor

Many people are unsure whether to make email submissions or queries. The simple answer to this question is, don't. Every magazine listed in the *Writers' and Artists' Yearbook* provides an email address, but this isn't an invitation to bombard the editorial desk with story ideas. You may not feel that your politely worded query is part of a bombardment but it will feel like that to the secretary or PA who has literally dozens of similar requests to wade through (in addition to all the usual Viagra ads and other junk that the rest of us also contend with). Traditional snail mail is best in this instance. When you have a track record or a relationship with the editor, then a very brief phone call at an early stage (maybe stage six of the 14 points on the previous pages) might be in order.

Photographs

The media is increasingly a visual business and photographs will definitely add to the attractiveness of your feature proposal. Don't send negatives. Glossy, high-contrast prints will do. Often you can just provide your editor with a list of possible illustrations and if they like the piece then they will ask for the photos to be sent as a jpeg attachment. Photos take up a lot of room on a PC however, so definitely wait until you're asked before you send them, and ensure you have checked what size and resolution is required. A digital camera is a cheap addition to a writer's armoury and, for the feature writer, should never be further away than the notebook.

If illustrations are more appropriate for your article, don't attempt to draw your own. Even if you are a talented artist it may well be that an editor prefers to use an in-house art department.

Payment

Fees vary hugely, depending on the circulation of the magazine. A well-known writer will claim a much higher fee than an unknown one. Fees may well increase once you become a regular contributor.

Here are some crucial don'ts:

- *Don't* preach.
- *Don't* pad. If your article isn't long enough, write it up for another magazine.
- *Don't* repeat yourself. Readers will lose interest unless every sentence is new.
- *Don't* be discouraged. Each rejection slip is a badge of bravery and should be received with pride.
- *Don't* be pessimistic. Upbeat people have more friends than negative people. And so it is with articles. No one wants to feel dejected at the end of a feature and so optimistic, positive pieces – like optimistic, positive people – have better chances.

Changes in printing technology mean there are a lot more niche and specialist magazines. And of course there are many internet magazines that invite contributions. All of which means that there are more outlets for good feature writers than ever before. This doesn't mean that it is easy to get your work out there. There are also more would-be writers than ever before. And many of them are putting their work on the net for free. Web content from films to music to literature is easy to get hold of for nothing. There is a whole generation of web-literate consumers who expect to pay little or nothing for material they find on the internet. I'll cover this in a little more detail in Chapter 8, 'Blogging'.

Insight

Don't neglect the web as a potential marketplace for your work. As years go by and the advertising business diverts more of its expenditure from traditional media, such as television, towards the web, then you'll find ad-supported websites looking to cherry-pick the best writers. The half-hearted bloggers will disappear from the web too. The cream of the talent will rise to the surface and will always be in demand.

Professional tip from Anthony Clavane

My tip would be to spend a long time on your intro. After that the rest of the feature should follow naturally. Many journalists talk about a good pay-off line – the last line of the piece – but I believe if you come to the end and you have a great pay-off line maybe substitute it for your intro. Very few people actually read the whole of an article. Which is sad but true.

Anthony Clavane is chief sports writer for the *Sunday Mirror*. His work has also been published in many other newspapers and magazines.

TEST YOUR KNOWLEDGE

Q1 What is the most important part of an article?

Q2 When do editors buy their Christmas articles?

Q3 How many specialist magazines are there in the UK?

Q4 What should your title be like?

Q5 How many years is it since the first Urdu language typewriter was produced?

4

The short story

In this chapter you will learn:
- *the scope of the modern short story*
- *some essential ingredients for a successful short story*
- *how to generate ideas for a good short story*
- *where to send your stories.*

> *A short story is like a slap in the face. It must immediately sting, make itself known at once, and it must leave a red mark for hours to come.*
>
> Martin Booth

In the preface to his book *The Modern Short Story*, H. E. Bates says that 'it is the most difficult and exacting of prose forms'. This is the accepted point of view and yet it is the form that beginners to writing are encouraged to attempt before going on to the long haul of the novel. And there's sense in this. All writers need to learn to write with economy, to draw a character in a few deft strokes of the pen and to pull a reader into a world. All writers need to learn about how to structure a piece that takes the reader on a journey. And there is nothing like finishing a piece to encourage a writer to move on and develop further.

Some common mistakes

The most common mistake is to try to be too dramatic. Thinking that a short story must be high impact, writers are drawn to violence and suffering. Novice writers often try and make an impression by shock. It's a tactic best avoided however. Everyone tends to recoil from an explosion and readers are no different when they see blood and guts spilled too visibly on to the page. They do what most people do: they avert their eyes. Unless a new writer is very skilled it will be hard to persuade a reader to be led down the darkest alleyways.

Another mistake is to offer up as a story the unaltered anecdote. If you have a job where you mix with a lot of people you are bound to have a fund of funny stories. But what works as a funny story at a party doesn't always work on the page. Similarly, we all know people who are great raconteurs in the pub or around a dinner-party table, but it does not follow that any of their tales would work in a written form without a great deal of revision.

The same is true of those writers who simply give us their unvarnished personal experiences, however shocking or powerful these have been. This is not to decry the value of writing these down. Often they can be the springboard for producing honed and developed pieces. And in any case making sense of our own lives is at least part of the point of writing. All writing.

However, there needs to be craft, care and thought in a written story. Readers are far more acute and unforgiving than an audience at a social gathering.

Insight

Even a very good anecdote doesn't have the power of a well-worked story when transferred directly to the page. It needs something more. It needs the application of craft.

The ingredients

To produce an interesting short story you will need:

▶ *an original idea*
▶ *believable characters*

▶ *a convincing background*
▶ *a good opening*
▶ *conflict*
▶ *suspense*
▶ *a sense of shape*
▶ *a satisfying ending.*

It's obvious, isn't it? And yet these ingredients are by no means always easy to find. And it's not like cooking. It's not like you can do without one of these, or find a simple, more accessible substitute.

Finding short story ideas

In Chapter 2 we talked about how ideas need to be hunted down and corralled. We owe it to ourselves to treat our ideas seriously and as important. You should, therefore, have lots of rough ideas in your notebook. You should have a file of odd incidents culled from local papers and magazines.

The germ of a short story could also come from an overheard conversation or a fragment of something that was on television or radio. Or you could try one of these exercises in order to generate still more ideas for short stories. They are both good ways of involving other people in your writing. The more involved they feel the more supportive they are likely to be and your life as a writer is likely to be much easier if your partner, friends and family all feel included in your efforts.

Exercise 15

Use secrets. This is a well-known exercise used by lots of writers and teachers to get the imagination going. It seems particularly suitable for the short story form.

You will need some close friends to help you. Better still the members of your writing group could help!

Everyone should now write down a secret which they fold up and place in a hat, a bag or a box. You should draw out a secret and use it as a springboard for a story. If you are doing this in a writing group you should all meet again and swap the stories you developed from each other's secrets.

Exercise 16

Use photographs. Whatever kind of writer you are it's a good idea to get into the habit of collecting photographs and postcards. Anything that grabs your eye should be snapped up and placed safe in a box somewhere. On a day when the ideas just don't seem to want to come, you can go to the box and pick out a photo at random. It's probably best to choose one that you collected such a long time ago that you had forgotten you'd got it.

Spend ten minutes free writing about the photograph. Now use the photo – or a detail from it – as a starting point for your story.

Finding believable characters

The most important task for the short story writer is to choose the right central character. Unlike a novel, a short story usually revolves around one person whose problem becomes increasingly interesting. The reader needs to know and care about this person and so it is probably helpful to restrict yourself to a single viewpoint throughout the story. In other words, see everything through one character's eyes. Make sure in choosing your character that *you* at least sympathize with their plight. If you don't, then it is unlikely that any of your readers will care either.

At this stage in your writing career it might be a good idea to write using the first person. Your readers are possibly more likely to identify more easily with an 'I' character.

Insight

Dialogue is essential in a short story. People reveal themselves by the things they say and readers will feel that they know your characters far better if they can hear their unique voices.

Short stories are where eccentrics can often find a suitable fictional home. Here is an exercise that has often been used very effectively at the Arvon Centre at Lumb Bank. It is an excellent one for finding characters and their voices.

Exercise 17

Take yourself off into your nearest town or village. Spend some time really looking at your fellow citizens. Find someone who is as different from yourself as you can. Someone much older, say. Or much younger. And follow them. Keep a discreet distance but stay close enough to be able to watch how they move. If they are with companions, try and overhear what they say. You could even begin this exercise in a café, overhearing what your fellow customers are talking about and then following a selected target as he or she leaves the premises. Try and gather as much information about your target's life as you can and then, safely back at home, make some detailed notes. This should give you enough material on which to base a central character.

A convincing background

Your characters should move in a realistic setting, though you don't want to spend a lot of time evoking it. Your job as a short story writer is to take your readers into the imaginary world and make them believe in it immediately.

It is probably a good idea to choose the kind of setting that you know well. And think about all the senses. Smells and sounds are as important as the way things look. And taste and touch can be as evocative too.

A good opening

A good short story needs to get going quickly. Your main character needs to make an appearance straightaway. You must arouse your reader's curiosity within the first page. Ideally, the first paragraph should be arresting. If the story doesn't really get going until page three, then throw away pages one and two. It might be that you as a writer need the first two pages, but the reader doesn't.

Here are three openings to contemporary short stories that show how it is done. The first is *Capacity* by the American writer Marjorie Sandor, who won the National Jewish Book Award in 2005.

> *By the time she was eleven, the house was deep in age-old quiet. She had tender breasts already and, my God, what looked like hips, said the Shapiro aunts, turning her this way and that in the kitchen. Her mother and the aunts kept her well-surrounded: no dark fact could break into this picture, dirty it up or confuse it. But it was 1936 and her father's store was in trouble, and something else was wrong. His eye-sight was failing, and he got up to pee five times a night. Nobody spoke of it. The aunts swarmed in her*

mother's parlor, clutching Clara to their bosoms, giving her big smacking kisses. 'Doll,' they called her, and 'Cutie-pie', words that didn't suit her then, that never would. She felt, at the time, shunned by life, as if it didn't think her worth the effort, and was deliberately keeping away.

The second is *Are These Actual Miles?* by Raymond Carver.

Fact is the car needs to be sold in a hurry, and Leo sends Toni out to do it. Toni is smart and has personality. She used to sell children's encyclopedias door-to-door. She signed him up, even though he didn't have kids. Afterward, Leo asked her for a date, and the date led to this. This deal has to be cash, and it has to be done tonight. Tomorrow somebody they owe might slap a lien on the car. Monday they'll be in court, home free – but word on them went out yesterday when their lawyer mailed the letters of intention. The hearing on Monday is nothing to worry about, the lawyer has said. They'll be asked some questions, and they'll sign some papers, and that's it. But sell the convertible, he said – today, tonight. They can hold on to the little car, Leo's car, no problem. But they go into court with that big convertible, the court will take it, and that's that.

And the third is the opening of Jo Verity's story *Think Like A Bee*. Jo Verity was the winner of the Richard and Judy short story competition in 2004.

Esther didn't recognize the elderly man standing at the door. A stranger on the step after dark would normally cause her heart to race but this one looked pretty harmless.

'Good evening, Mrs Feldman. Esther.' Well, he certainly knew who she was. 'I was in the neighbourhood and I recalled that your house was on Jenckes Street. So I figured that if I knocked on every sixth door, the probability was that I'd track you down sooner or later. I only had to call at nine houses. Not bad.' He paused and whilst she wrestled

with the mathematics of the door-to-door enquiry, he
added 'It's Stanley. Stanley Johnson? Thanksgiving Day?
Remember?'

A recollection lay buried somewhere in her memory but,
before she had time to dig it out the draught from the open
door caught the curtains and they billowed out, flicking a
vase of crimson gladioli off the window ledge in the living
room. The two of them knelt, gathering up broken glass,
mopping up stale water, and she was grateful that this little
guy, whoever he was, had turned up out of the blue.

All three of these openings entice a reader into a compelling,
imaginative world and hint at dramas still to come.

Exercise 18

> Reread the openings above. Select one and try and write the
> next paragraph. When you are in the library next, see if you can
> read the story to see how close you were. Did the story move
> in unexpected directions? Copying a writer's style directly like
> this can be a good way to learn. You may even prefer your next
> paragraph, which will be quite a confidence boost!

CONFLICT

'Happiness writes white' they say. In other words, contentment
rarely makes for powerful stories. In a piece of short fiction you will
need to ensure that your characters face problems from the start.
They should be beset with difficulties and enemies and conflict.

Insight

These difficulties needn't be melodramatic – it could be as
simple as someone occupying your character's favourite

(Contd)

seat in the local pub – but it should disturb them and disrupt their rhythm.

Here is an exercise from the American Orange prize-winner Suzanne Berne and it's designed to allow you to develop conflict without succumbing to the temptation to become overblown.

Exercise 19

Describe a ritual that you have. Everyone has rituals, things they do to control their environment. It might be the way that you make tea, or a routine you have when going to work. Something you do in more or less the same order at more or less the same time. Now imagine a break in that routine. What happens if the kettle doesn't work? Or a bus breaks down? Imagine the chain of events that might develop from there. Then imagine that you meet the person who has caused this disruption in your day. What might happen then? It's a good exercise for making it clear how small events can produce big emotional conflict.

Shape

Put simply this means that your story should have a beginning, a middle and an end. The beginning sets the scene, introduces the characters and poses the problem. The middle develops the action and explores the world of the story; and the end resolves the dilemmas of the central characters, for better or worse. Your task is to make sure that everything is relevant. Make sure that everything that might be irrelevant to the development of the story is jettisoned. Be hard on yourself and on your story.

SUSPENSE

Your story should be plausible but never predictable. Having
hooked your readers with a powerful or beguiling opening, you
need to prevent them wriggling off. Avoid the temptation to depart
from your main storyline or to get sucked into giving away too
much back story about your characters. You might need to know
where they went to school or how they met their first boyfriend
but, unless it's absolutely essential to the story, your reader
probably doesn't. It's about building tension: making the reader
worry about what will happen next.

A good way to sketch out a plot is to keep building on that first
dramatic scene. Each scene should suggest another. A lot of
writers plan their plots in advance before they write a word.
And it's probably sensible. You should also give your characters
choices as the story progresses. Different roads to take. Sometimes
these should be the wrong roads. Your reader should want to
scream at your characters, or to shake them. We should fall in
love with some, and be irritated by others, but feel at least a little
sympathy for all of them. A good way to think about constructing
a storyline is to imagine that your job as a writer is to get your
characters stuck up a tree, to throw rocks at them and then to get
them down again.

We'll return to the importance of a strong storyline later in this
book, but its impact can't be overestimated. It is, after all, the story
that keeps readers interested rather than your beautiful prose.
Every paragraph, every line, should move the story along. If it
doesn't do that it hasn't earned its place, however euphonic it is.

A satisfying ending

This doesn't need to be a happy one. Nor does it have to be one
that ties up all the characters' relationships. It is perfectly possible

to have a well-written, satisfying ending that leaves the possibilities open. With all stories it is important that you leave the reader some of the work to do. Readers are smart and want to be able to guess what is going to happen to the characters. As the story progresses you will want to wrong-foot them and surprise them. But resist the temptation at the end to tell them everything that happens to the characters. Leave them to reflect and to wonder about the characters' futures. You don't necessarily have to have a dramatic twist either. That can look contrived. Unless it is very skilfully done it will just irritate a reader. While your story should end with some sort of emotional release for the reader, try to avoid doing this with a death. If you kill off your viewpoint character, then the reader will be disconcerted by wondering who is telling the story. And if you kill off the hero, or a character that the reader has come to like or to identify with, then you cause a little death in the heart of the reader too.

As a general rule, when deaths occur in short stories they should happen at the beginning rather than the end.

Exercise 20

Choose a theme and central character for a short story. Make notes for a beginning, a middle and an end and write the first 500 words. You should by now have some substantial material from previous exercises.

Where to send your story

In the first place you should send your completed short story to a drawer. Print it off and leave it to sit and simmer for several weeks. While your story is lying apparently dormant in that drawer it will actually be cooking somewhere in your subconscious. When you do finally return to it, you will be amazed by how many flaws you find. Don't be depressed or downhearted by this. It's a necessary part of the process. Read your story through carefully, making notes in the margin. Always, always, always edit from a hard copy. Don't try and edit on-screen. You'll miss things. The experience of reading on-screen is very different from reading a printed page and it makes sense to come to your work in the same way that your reader will.

Once you've edited and revised and – probably – completely redrafted I would send it back to the drawer to simmer some more and then take it out and go through the editing, revising and redrafting process all over again. You might want to do this a few times.

When you are finally happy with your story you can start finding outlets for it. Don't feel nervous about this. You've worked hard on your story. If you've followed all the advice and exercises in this chapter then you have worked very hard indeed, and a tale that you have grown, developed and nurtured over all these weeks and months deserves a readership. It is very possible, likely even, that the first few stories you send out will attract rejections, but remember that we are choosing to see these as scars and battle-honours, necessary bruises on the way to ultimate success.

MAGAZINES

The best place to look for outlets is the *Writers' and Artists' Yearbook* (A & C Black Publishers Limited), which contains the addresses of more or less anyone a writer might ever find useful, including those magazines who publish short stories.

I have, however, included a few of the major magazines here. All of these also accept poetry. Once again it makes sense to study the magazine before you submit your work.

Aesthetica
PO Box 371
York YO23 1WL
Tel: 01904 479168
Email: info@aestheticamagazine.com
Website: www.aestheticamagazine.com
Editor: Cherie Federico

Ambit
17 Priory Gardens
London N6 5QY
Website: www.ambitmagazine.co.uk
Editor: Martin Bax

Mslexia
PO Box 656
Newcastle Upon Tyne NE99 1PZ
Tel: 0191 261 6636
Email: postbag@mslexia.demon.co.uk
Website: www.mslexia.co.uk

Stand
School of English, University of Leeds
Leeds LS2 9JT
Tel: 0113 233 4794
Website: www.standmagazine.org
Managing editor: Jon Glover

Staple
114–16 St Stephen's Road
Nottingham NG2 4JS
Website: www.staplemagazine.wordpress.com
Editor: Wayne Burrows

There are two publishers in this country who specialize in the short story – look out for their anthologies and subscribe to their newsletters so that you know when they are asking for submissions:

Comma press
3rd Floor, 24 Lever Street, Northern Quarter
Manchester M1 1DW
Website: www.commapress.co.uk

Salt publishing
PO Box 937, Great Wilbraham
Cambridge CB1 5JX
Website: www.saltpublishing.com

THE SHORT STORY COMPETITION

Despite the dedicated work by editors like Ra Page at Comma and Chris Hamilton-Emory at Salt, the fact remains that there are only a handful of short story outlets, their editors often drowning in manuscripts and physically unable to read each one, never mind publish them all. One online monthly magazine restricts its writers to one published story every three years in order to spread around the opportunities it offers!

One place where your work can be read is the short story competition. There are lots of these now, with prizes ranging from a few pounds to several thousands of pounds, and it can be a practical way to test how your writing is progressing. Writers should be collecting rejection slips the way that Prussian officers collected duelling scars, and short story writers should approach competitions in the same way. Winning is only part of the point; their real function is to stimulate you to produce new work.

This is not the same as urging you to send in any old thing. Each competition is a mountain to be conquered and, as a mountaineer setting out on a new expedition, it pays to be thoroughly and properly prepared.

Not all competitions are the same
Some are simple fundraisers for the organizers while others carry considerable weight and heft. Winning the Bridport prize, for

example, gave Kate Atkinson a great deal of enhanced standing in the literary world.

When entering a competition make sure that you research the judges too. Try and read some of their work. If you can't muster any enthusiasm for their work at all then there has to be a fair chance that you and they are not on the same wavelength.

Some competitions use a filter system, where the named judges only select from a shortlist chosen by others. If the competition is being held by a writers' group, and many of the smaller ones are, then it is very likely that the filter judges will be drawn from that group. It makes sense therefore to check out the group. How long has it been established? How many members does it have? Have they published any group pamphlets or anthologies? If so it might be a good idea to have a look at the kind of work they produce.

Certainly you absolutely must get hold of any anthologies of winning and short-listed entries from previous competitions. This is the best way to see what the standard is and whether or not it is worth the outlay.

It is also a form of good manners. You want people to read your stories, so it is only right to read the work of those who have successfully gone before. And, as I keep saying throughout this book, reading is the quickest way to improve as a writer. One of the great things about writing is that we can choose our own mentors. It doesn't even matter if they are dead! We can study their works and learn at the knee of the masters (and mistresses) of the craft at our leisure.

It ought to go without saying, but read the competition rules and entry forms carefully, do exactly what they ask and double-check before you post off the entry. Check the small print too. Make sure that copyright eventually returns to the author, even if the competition organizers have copyright for a short while in order to use the piece in an anthology or for publicity purposes, which is fair enough.

Don't try and amend your entry after you have submitted it. There's really no point. If the story doesn't get placed, redo it with the corrections and amendments for another competition at another time.

Here is a list of the major regular short story competitions, but there are others springing up all the time. Keep an eye on magazines like *Mslexia* (it's ostensibly just for women but I would argue that all writers should consider a subscription to this magazine) that produce a regular list of competitions. In addition, The Book Trust provides a comprehensive A–Z of annual awards and prizes. Visit www.booktrust.org.uk.

Major short story competitions include the following:

The Bridport Prize
Bridport Arts Centre, South Street, Bridport
Dorset DT6 3NR
Website: www.bridportprize.org.uk
Short story and poetry categories. Closes end of June each year.
Prize: £5,000

Fish Short Story Prize
Fish Publishing, Durrus, Bantry
Co. Cork, Republic of Ireland
Email: info@fishpublishing.com
Website: www.fishpublishing.com
Prize: 10,000 euros

The Lady Short Story Competition
The Lady, 39–40 Bedford Street
London WC2E 9ER
Open to anyone, details are published in an issue of _The Lady_.
First prize: £1,000

Bryan Macmahon Short Story Award
Writers' Week, 24 The Square, Listowel
Co. Kerry, Republic of Ireland
Tel: (353) 6821074
Email: info@writersweek.ie
Website: www.writersweek.ie
Prize: 2,000 euros

National Short Story Prize
Booktrust, Bookhouse, 45 East Hill
London SW18 2QZ
Email: Hannah@booktrust.org.uk
Website: www.theshortstory.org.uk/prizes
A prize of £15,000 is awarded for the winning story, plus £3,000
for the runner-up and £500 for the three other shortlisted stories.
Please note that entrants must be published authors.

The Tom-Gallon Trust Award and the Olive Cook Prize
Awards Secretary, The Society of Authors
84 Drayton Gardens,
London SW10 9SB
Tel: 020 7373 6642
Email: info@societyofauthors.org
Website: www.societyofauthors.org

An award of £1,000 is made on the basis of a submitted short story to fiction writers of limited means who have had at least one short story accepted for publication. Both awards are biennial and awarded in alternate years.

Closing date 31 October each year.

Professional tip from Jo Verity

Start as near to the end of your story as possible. No waffle about blue skies and buzzing bees – unless they sting someone. Draw your reader in quickly with dialogue or an interesting observation. Assume an 'intelligent reader'. Don't hand everything to them on a plate. Make them do some of the work – they'll feel more committed. When you think you've finished, try knocking off the last sentence. If the story still works, why is it there?

In addition to her prize-winning short stories, Jo Verity is the author of the novels *Bells* and *Sweets from Morocco* (both Honno).

10 THINGS TO REMEMBER

1 *Short stories aren't easier than novels just because they are shorter!*

2 *The advice you were given at school that a short story should have a clear beginning, middle and end is still relevant now.*

3 *Begin as close to the end of your story as you can.*

4 *A short story should describe an emotional journey. Your characters should change as a result of the events described in it.*

5 *If in doubt, begin with dialogue – it gives immediacy and pace.*

6 *There is no need to provide a twist in the end of the tale. Leaving the readers with a wry smile or an ache is better than dazzling them with your cleverness.*

7 *Research short story competitions before you enter them.*

8 *The first place to send your story is to the drawer. Let it ferment a while.*

9 *Beware of giving too much back story about your characters. You might need to know everything about them, but your readers don't.*

10 *Learn from modern practitioners as well as the old masters. Start with Kate Atkinson, Ian McEwan, A. L. Kennedy, Nicholas Royle, Alison Macleod and Tessa Hadley.*

5

··

Poetry

In this chapter you will learn:
- *how to find your voice*
- *how to experiment in different forms*
- *when to send your poetry out*
- *where to send it.*

> *Poetry lifts the veil from the hidden beauty of the world, and makes familiar objects be as if they were not familiar.*
>
> Percy Bysshe Shelley

_____

Finding your own voice

Of all forms of writing, poetry is perhaps the most natural, but also the one most hedged around with rules. Everyone writes a kind of poetry at some time in their lives. At school it is almost the very first thing that we are encouraged to do. Almost as soon as they've got us to write our names, they are setting us the task of writing 'poems' about 'Spring' or 'Christmas' or 'Snow' or 'My Mum'. As kids we set to with a will, spinning words into shapes that sound good. Children love rhyme and rhythm and the startling image: all the things that make language memorable. And they can do it almost instinctively. It is for this reason that some writing by primary-age children can be so charming and so powerful. Of course it can also be banal and trite and, like certain children themselves, capable of being loved only by its creator. (Or its creator's mother.) The point is that children are rarely earnest about writing poetry and are happy to create unusual linguistic constructions merely because they like the sound of the words.

It is this spirit of mischief and play that we should be aiming for as poets. One of the tragedies of the school system is that it seems designed to eradicate playfulness from writing. It's one of the things that we have to relearn. Writing should be play. It shouldn't be a chore and it shouldn't be a job. We should be absorbed in our writing, lost in it the way that children lose themselves in a game. With any luck the hours will pass quickly, and we will find ourselves exhausted but content.

Of course, after childhood poems come the tortured outpourings of adolescence. Nearly everybody has teenage poems in the back of a drawer somewhere. Or did once. This is likely to be a kind of emotional diary fuelled by hormones and rage. It is a more effective way of dealing with unhappiness than drink or drugs or self-harm, but often comes from the same source. Poetry from this period of our lives can be a cry for help, or a way of dealing with emotional distress. It is often raw and unshaped, the playfulness of childhood being replaced by the self-regard of adolescence, but still there is often an absence of self-consciousness that means pieces written during this period can have real power. Mature writers can come upon poems that they wrote in this period and be shocked by the vividness and genuine force of their writing, even while wincing at some of the sentiments.

Adolescence can also be a time when people are reading poetry, either because they have to at school, or because they are looking for writers who can best express their inner chaos.

A lot of the poetry we read at school is from way back in the past. Some lucky students will have had teachers who pointed them towards Philip Larkin, Sharon Olds, Sylvia Plath, Simon Armitage or Carol Ann Duffy, but others, fed a diet of Andrew Marvell or Gerard Manley Hopkins, are alienated and think poetry is stuffy and not for them.

The problem often comes when, as adults, people want to express themselves through poetry and find that the only models they have are from several generations, even centuries, ago. Reading these masters, it can feel impossible to imagine emulating them by writing poetry of your own. It can seem too difficult, or a job for those with a particular kind of education.

The former poet laureate Ted Hughes once wrote to his daughter, Frieda (also a fine poet), that the only way for anyone to improve their own poetry was to read the works of others aloud.

As new poets, what we need to do is to try and bring back the spirit of play. To tap into the child we were, or the adolescent we were, and to see if we can do now what we did without thinking back then. And we're going to start small. Very small.

Haiku

A haiku is a three-line poem which tries to preserve a fleeting moment. It acts as an emotional photograph of something that has passed the moment the poet tried to capture it. There's a sense that every writer writes anticlockwise: i.e. tries to hold back time, to cage it, which is both impossible and a writer's duty. There is, as the American poet and undertaker Thomas Lynch writes, 'No such thing as still life' and yet we persist in the attempt to hold the moment by writing it down.

The melancholy that surrounds a good haiku is a result of the tension between the necessity of the poet's attempt to create something lasting out of what must soon pass away, and the futility of that attempt.

In the original Japanese tradition the haiku was a poem of 17 syllables (5–7–5), though you may want to vary this just a little. Remember, the point is to *play*.

Here are some examples of traditional haiku:

> *The thief*
> *Left it behind –*
> *The moon at the window*

Ryokan

A brushwood gate,
And for a lock –
This snail

Basho

In the dense mist
What is being shouted
Between hill and boat?

Isso

And here are two modern haiku:

Water piccolos,
Snowdrops sounding out their song,
Dancing trees in wind

Adam Horovitz

In the lonely valley
the wind reminds
the drying shirt to wave

Peter Mortimer

And a very famous 19-syllable effort from Ezra Pound:

The apparition of these faces in the crowd:
Petals on a wet, black bough.

Exercise 21

Try writing a haiku – or a series of them – that expresses how you feel at the end of a holiday.

Sonnets

This is an ancient fixed form most famously used by Shakespeare and still much used today. It is good training for the aspiring poet, both because the form is a simple one and because it is extremely hard to pull off successfully. Here is one of Shakespeare's best-known sonnets.

> *My mistress' eyes are nothing like the sun;*
> *Coral is far more red, than her lips red;*
> *If snow be white, why then her breasts are dun;*
> *If hairs be wires, black wires grow on her head.*
> *I have seen roses damasked, red and white,*
> *But no such roses see I in her cheeks;*
> *And in some perfumes is there more delight*
> *Than in the breath that from my mistress reeks.*
> *I love to hear her speak, yet well I know*
> *That music hath a far more pleasing sound:*
> *I grant I never saw a goddess go,*
> *My mistress, when she walks, treads on the ground:*
> *And yet by heaven, I think, my love as rare,*
> *As any she belied with false compare.*

Shakespeare here pokes fun at the poets of his time and the convention of praising their loved ones in extravagant, even ridiculous, terms.

You'll notice that there are 14 lines, with the rhyme scheme abab/cdcd/efef/gg.

Each line has ten syllables, with the stress on the second syllable of each pair. This is iambic pentameter, the natural form of spoken English. You don't need to worry about the technical term;

you'll find that you often do it naturally in ordinary speech. It's the heartbeat of the English language.

Each sonnet has a single theme and in writing your own work it is probably best to stick to one defining idea.

Here is a modern sonnet by Ros Barber.

'How to Leave the World that Worships Should' by Ros Barber

Let faxes butter-curl on dusty shelves
Let junkmail build its castles in the hush
of other people's halls. Let deadlines burst
and flash like glorious fireworks somewhere else.
As hours go softly by, let others curse
the roads where distant drivers queue like sheep.
Let e-mails fly like panicked, tiny birds.
Let phones, unanswered, ring themselves to sleep.
Above, the sky unrolls its telegram,
immense and wordless, simply understood:
you've made your mark like birdtracks in the sand –
now make the air in your lungs your livelihood.
See how each wave arrives at last to heave
itself upon the beach and vanish. Breathe.

From the *Herne Bay* sonnets. Published in *Material* (Anvil)

Exercise 22

Try writing your own sonnet now. It can be a love poem in the traditional manner, or about something quite different in the way that Ros Barber's piece is. It'll take you some time and you may not be satisfied with the results, but it will be a stimulating exercise and should be enjoyable in the way that crosswords are, even if in the end you don't feel that what you've done compares well with Bill Shakespeare's.

Free verse

Most traditional verse forms have strict rules designed to force a poet to be creative rather than to go for the obvious. If you are forced to go for a word with a certain number of syllables then you are often driven away from your comfort zone and your usual vocabulary and into a more interesting place.

The great American poet Robert Frost said that 'writing free verse is like playing tennis with the net down'. By which he meant that it was without challenge or skill. Nevertheless it has become the dominant form of contemporary poetry, with the poet's theme being developed in a conversational style. Here is a classic poem by William Carlos Williams that seems a relatively small step on from the haiku. Its importance seems to lie in demonstrating that ordinary language can have profundity.

'This is Just to Say' by William Carlos Williams

I have eaten
the plums
that were in
the icebox
and which
you were probably
saving
for breakfast
Forgive me
they were delicious
so sweet
and so cold

This is a poem that intrigues almost everybody who reads it, for reasons that aren't immediately clear. It seems to hint at something just behind the words that we can't quite catch. It also seems to do very well what Shelley asked of poetry, in that it makes the familiar strange again.

Exercise 23

Imagine that you are the owner of the plums. Write a reply to William Carlos Williams using the same style he does. Try and use the same number of syllables and the same line breaks. There is nothing wrong with imitation as a method of learning. Often in the gap between the original and the imitation, something new and unforeseen emerges.

Next is an exercise from the award-winning poet Jean Sprackland. It's a good way of returning us to that sense of playing with words which we had as children, while at the same time getting us used to the idea that if it is any good, free verse is usually not as free as all that. There are usually constraints on the poet, even if they are self-imposed.

Exercise 24

Write the word 'autumn' on a blank piece of paper. Underneath list all the words that come to mind when you think of autumn. Spend a good five minutes doing this.

Now produce a poem that does not include any of the words in your list.

After you have tackled the exercise above, see how the poet
Iain Crichton Smith has done it below.

'Autumn' by Iain Crichton Smith

Autumn reminds one
of heavy wardrobes,
large and mahogany,
and of coalsheds
with frosty locks on them.
It reminds one
of tenements
with broken windows
and dogs running through puddles
to windy appointments.
It reminds one
of postmen
humping their bags
over fences and ditches
towards a spectral house.
It reminds one
of Charity Shops
with suits and shirts,
blouses and skirts,
and books from dimmed authors.
It reminds one
of those who have left
to seek new countries
and who gaze into glasses
thinking of the old one.
In autumn
children play with a coloured ball
beside the sea
where the sand rises behind them
in a fragile statue.

From *A Country for Old Men* (Carcanet)

Writing poetry for yourself

No one writes poetry to become rich or famous. Probably the majority of poets don't even write for publication. Most poets write to make sense of the world, or to celebrate people, places, events or emotions that are particularly important to them. It's a powerful, almost primeval, impulse and its importance can be judged by the fact that at the most important of human moments – birth, love, death – people always reach for poetry. At heightened moments, heightened language is called for.

Here are three short poems that record each of these important rites of passage, each of which could be a trigger for your own personal memories and could spur you into writing the poem that only you can write. The first is one of mine about the difficult birth of my youngest child. I have never tried to publish it before now. It was enough that it seemed to fix the experience for me.

'Surprise Party' by Stephen May

You weren't born so much as choked on:
coughed up and purple-black, translucent.
A half-sucked sweet. Plainly not ready for us,
the way that we were ready for you.
You were unmoved by the fanfare of bleeps,
the symphony of curses
from the handsome Slovak nurse.
The collision of panic and jargon
so familiar from Saturday night television.
You slept through it all while
I rehearsed funerals and teary phone calls and
cancelled everything.
When you deigned to cry
it was half-hearted, fitful,
as resentful as a schoolboy kept behind without cause. You were

unimpressed by all the sudden laughter
and high-fiving,
irritated by the giggles that fizzed into the ward
like Cava.

As we saw with the haiku, often one simple image can trigger off reflections on a number of issues. In the following poem Patience Agbabi uses the memory of a trip to the London Eye to reflect upon the state of a relationship.

'The London Eye' by Patience Agbabi

Through my gold-tinted Gucci sun-glasses,
the sightseers. Big Ben's quarter chime
strikes the convoy of number 12 buses
that bleeds into the city's monochrome.
Through somebody's zoom lens, me shouting
to you, 'Hell...on...bridge...'minister!'
The aerial view postcard, the man writing
squat words like black cabs in rush hour.
The South Bank buzzes with a rising treble.
You kiss my cheek, formal as a blind date.
We enter Cupid's Capsule, a thought bubble
where I think, 'Space age!', you think, 'She was late.'
Big Ben strikes six, my SKIN. Beat blinks, replies
18.02. We're moving anti-clockwise.

Exercise 25

You could try writing a poem with this structure about somewhere that has a personal significance to you. Note that this poem is written in the present tense as though it is all happening right now. Also pay attention to Patience Agbabi's use of rhyme. She is particularly good at using half-rhymes (the technical term for this is assonance) such as *glasses* and *buses* and *treble* and *bubble*.

A WORD ABOUT RHYME

When most people think about poetry they think about rhyme. In particular they think about rhyming couplets or other simple end-rhymes, but the world of contemporary poetry is not keen on end-rhymes. Rhyme is still a weapon in the poet's armoury but it is to be used sparingly and in surprising ways. You are much more likely to find modern poets using rhyme within their lines, or breaking up their lines so that the rhyme is not immediately obvious. There is a good reason for this. It is hard to create end-rhymes that are fresh and original or that don't seem contrived. They can also unbalance a poem so that the ending of each line assumes exaggerated importance.

Here is a poem that uses end-rhymes particularly cleverly, with cunning and subtlety, even if the poem itself is mildly depressing.

'Home Is So Sad' by Philip Larkin

Home is so sad. It stays as it was left,
Shaped to the comfort of the last to go
As if to win them back. Instead, bereft
Of having anyone to please, it withers so,
Having no heart to put aside the theft
And turn again to what it started as,
A joyous shot at how things ought to be,
Long fallen wide. You can see how it was:
Look at the pictures and the cutlery.
The music in the piano stool. That vase.

From *The Whitsun Weddings* (Faber and Faber)

Reading poetry

It is said, and only half-jokingly, that there are far more poets than there are readers of poetry these days. It is true that poetry has fallen away from its position as the foremost of the written art forms. Since the advent of recorded music many people turn to song lyrics to find memorable words that express their emotions at important times in their lives. Pop music has replaced many of the functions of poetry. Nevertheless there is a thriving poetry scene in the UK, nurtured by bodies like the Poetry Society (see 'Taking it further'), and there are many more poetry readings than there ever used to be. As with all writing, it is only by reading widely and deeply in our chosen forms that we really improve. Unfortunately most bookshops only stock books by a few well-known poets and not many of them either. Libraries are better. And there are, of course, a wide range of magazines catering for all types of poetry.

POETRY READINGS

Listening to poets read can give us a completely new slant on their work. Often what has seemed difficult or obscure can become suddenly clear when we hear a poet's personal emphasis and stress. Reading out loud is also a great way to get a sense of whether your own poetry is working. Even if there is no one else listening there is something about hearing your work that makes you become suddenly alive to mistakes, clunky phrases, poor word choices and faulty rhythms. And the act of reading aloud seems to suggest replacements almost immediately.

Exercise 26

Take one of the poems you have written in previous exercises and read it aloud. Now make any changes you think are necessary. There will almost certainly be some and your work will almost certainly improve.

Unlikely points of view

Poets are in the business of making their own world make sense, if only for a moment. It is no surprise then, to find that many can be self-absorbed. That is their job in a way. But it can be useful practice to step outside the self and try and look at everyday objects in an unusual way. One technique is to write from the point of view of someone, or even something, totally removed from your everyday life.

In this poem Clare Shaw writes as though she were a bus shelter reflecting on its life.

'Poem from a Bus Shelter' by Clare Shaw

This is not a life, but if it was
I'd say I always lived here.
I'd say this street: this long grey face
of factories, flats; the boarded shops;
the tired, concrete houses, squats –
they saw my first bright day.
I was as clean as a breeze,
as cold as glass, I sweated rain,
was slicked by the wind, was beautifully bare.
I filled myself with city sound,
the blur and swirl of good blue air.
When Winter came, and the gale,
And the church roof flapped and fractured like a wing;
when thin trees fell
and shop fronts swelled and bellied –
I stood my ground.
I knew where I belonged.
I was the colour of a dockside warehouse,
blue-grey. The shade of a cold,
an evening cloud, a hangover, a foggy day.
If I had ever had a life
I would say that I was proud
and it could be true.
Come rain or snow,
come the long white corridor
of Christmas;

come crowds with spiteful corners; come
the wet green growl of winter spit;
come fist; come kick;
come the lurch of stolen cars;
come stone; come brick;
come I luv Gaz, Mick,
Shaz; come weekend chips;
come drunken piss; come empty cans;
come the sad pink skins of condoms,
dog shit, sick, come sick –
come morning, I was there.
And if I had ever had a life
half worth the privilege of the name –
if I had not been rooted to this spot
and treated to the things
that other lives spit out
I would be proud
and I would write it –
I would write it clear and loud
in bold black hand
I would write it.
I woz ere.

From *Straight Ahead* (Bloodaxe)

Exercise 27

A great way of generating new work is to find an object
from your own home and write from its point of view.
Think carefully about the function of your object and
what it might have seen in its life. What might the future
hold for it?

(This is an idea that is taken to a beautiful extreme in the
novel *The Collector Collector* by Tibor Fischer which is
narrated entirely by a Sumerian vase.)

Curses

These can be great fun, as the poem below by Ian Duhig
demonstrates. They provide a chance to use humour while venting
your wrath on things and people that annoy you. Try and come up
with the most exaggerated and exotic curses to heap on the heads
of those deserving these terrible fates. Read Ian's poem below
about losing his pen while teaching a poetry course at a writing
centre in the Yorkshire village of Heptonstall.

'A Curse for Heptonstall' by Ian Duhig

Come all you poets hear this call
Then bless this curse on Heptonstall
Where Parker Pens aren't safe at all
For stuffed with thieves is Heptonstall
O may my couplets never pall
Before well-cursed is Heptonstall
For every ill I'll cast a trawl
And dump the catch on Heptonstall
That all the bugs that fly or crawl
May swarm and pester Heptonstall
And tigers, bears and werewolves howl
For human flesh round Heptonstall
May drunken Scotsmen shout and brawl
Along the streets of Heptonstall
While madness-fits like those of Saul
Afflict the police of Heptonstall
And hydrophobic dingoes prowl
The nurseries of Heptonstall
While fire and brimstone showers fall
Upon the roofs of Heptonstall
And mortar rot from every wall
That holds a roof in Heptonstall
May shingles wrap him like a shawl
Who stole my pen in Heptonstall
O queue you fiends in Tophets hall
For outside duty in Heptonstall

My verse has now begun to stall
Take your turn on Heptonstall
No torment either large or small
Forget to hurl on Heptonstall
That chancrous Pennine caul
Of scurf, black Heptonstall
Where pens get stole.

From Singing Brink (Arvon Press)

Exercise 28

Try and use poetry to curse something, someone or somewhere. Make your invective as startling and as powerful as you can.

When is a poem finished?

Somebody once said that poems 'aren't finished, they're abandoned'. And it's true that you could tinker with your work for months or years without it ever seeming quite perfect. I do suggest that when you think you have got an acceptable draft just put it away in a drawer for at least a few days. It is amazing just how many changes will suggest themselves to you when you revisit the piece later. Some poems will need to go through many drafts, while others will come together quite rapidly, but in the end only you will know whether you have done enough work on a poem, whether it is the very best that you can do. One Irish poet said to me that since poems were usually so much shorter than other forms of writing, we really owed it to all other writers to make sure that we worked and reworked them properly. This is the same poet who recalled his wife coming home and asking him how his day had gone. He had been pleased to be able to reply 'Good news! I got rid of three words today.'

On the other hand you don't want to linger too long over one piece of work; there are other poems to write. I once asked a famous poet how he managed to produce a collection every year when others seemed to leave an ice age between new books. His answer was, 'You should ask the others what they actually do with their time. Poems are only short, aren't they?'

Having a trusted candid reader, or members of a writing group, appraise your work can be very useful too. And the aforementioned Poetry Society will, for a modest fee, find established poets to produce critiques of your work.

Sending your work out

It should go without saying that you don't send your work out to a magazine you haven't even read. That just seems rude as well as pointless. It seems reasonable to become a subscriber to a few poetry magazines before you attempt to become a contributor to them. You should be familiar with the standard and style of the poems in a magazine before you send your own work. Don't be too disillusioned if your work seems very different from what they usually print. A fresh voice and an unusual approach to writing is your biggest asset. Editors are desperate to find good new writers that they can champion in their pages. The trouble is that they are often overwhelmed by hundreds, even thousands, of mediocre poems. No wonder that so many reputable magazines are starting to rely on recommendations from creative writing tutors, or other established poets, rather than trawling through the thousands of submissions that arrive on their desks daily.

TITLES

A good, unusual title will usually ensure that an editor is intrigued enough to want to start reading and a good, arresting opening line is important too.

PRACTICALITIES

Send your target editor three or four poems, clearly typed, on one
sheet of A4 paper and make sure you include your name and contact
details; then wait. If you get a rejection letter, print the poems out
again and send them off to the next magazine on your list.

POETRY MAGAZINES

Here are some of the leading poetry magazines. All will have slightly
different submission guidelines so check these on the internet, by
email or by phone before sending off your work. Most literary
magazines are on very tight budgets so make sure that you include the
right postage and enclose an SAE if you want your work returned.

Acumen
6, The Mount, Higher Furzeham, Brixham
Devon TQ5 8BY
Tel: 01803 851098
Email: patricia@acumen-poetry.co.uk
Website: www.acumen-poetry.co.uk
Editor: Patricia Oxley

Agenda
The Wheelwrights, Fletching Street
Mayfield, East Sussex TN20 6TL
Tel: 01435 873703
Email: editor@agendapoetry.co.uk
Website: www.agendapoetry.co.uk
Editor: Patricia McCarthy

Blithe Spirit
Journal of the British Haiku Society
12 Eliot Vale, Blackheath
London SE3 0UW
Tel: 01547 528542
Website: www.britishhaikusociety.org
Editor: Graham High

The North
The Poetry Business
Bank Street Arts
32–40 Bank Street
Sheffield S1 2DS
Tel: 0114 346 3037
Website: www.poetrybusiness.co.uk
Editors: Peter Sansom and Janet Fisher

Orbis
17 Greenhow Avenue, West Kirby
Wirral CH48 5EL
Tel: 0151 625 1446
Email: carolebaldock@hotmail.com
Website: www.poetrymagazines.org
Editor: Carole Baldock

Smiths Knoll
Goldings, Goldings Lane, Leiston
Suffolk IP16 4EB
Tel: 01728 830631
Email: michael.laskey@ukonline.co.uk
Website: www.michael-laskey.co.uk/smiths_knoll.php
Editors: Michael Laskey and Joanna Cutts

Weyfarers
1 Mountside
Guildford
Surrey GU2 4JD
Email: weyfarers@yahoo.co.uk
Website: www.weyfarers.com
Editors: Martin Jones, Stella Stocker and Jeffrey Wheatley

Professional tip from Jacob Polley

I'm a great believer in routine: don't wait for inspiration to strike, but sit down every day at the same time, even if it's just for ten minutes, and WRITE. There is something about this kind of regular practice that helps swing open the gates between the unconscious mind and the rational self. You must be able to travel to and from both places if you want to produce work that will out-live the moment of its creation.

Jacob Polley is the author of *The Brink* and *Little Gods* (Picador).

If you want more information on how to write and publish poetry you should read *Write Poetry And Get It Published* by John Hartley-Williams and Matthew Sweeney.

10 THINGS TO REMEMBER

1 *Remember, poetry is at least as much about play as it is about anything else. Keep a sense of joy and wonder.*

2 *Ancient forms like sonnets or haiku can have resonance in the modern world.*

3 *Be ruthless in eliminating clichéd ideas or imagery from your poetry.*

4 *Find a good title.*

5 *Find an even better first line.*

6 *Be careful when using end-rhymes. It's much harder than you think.*

7 *If you get stuck try an unlikely point of view.*

8 *When you get the urge to write a poem read one first.*

9 *Just send out three or four poems at a time.*

10 *Keep reading (and hearing!) new poets.*

6

Creative non-fiction

In this chapter you will learn:
- *what creative non-fiction is*
- *how to find a subject*
- *how to think about structure*
- *how to write a proposal.*

Memoirs: The backstairs of history.

George Meredith

What is creative non-fiction?

Creative non-fiction is becoming the most widely used term to cover memoir, biography, autobiography, travel writing and writing about historical events. All these kinds of writing have always been popular, but in recent years there has been an increase in demand for works in these genres. More than ever, audiences seem to crave 'authenticity' and 'real life'. The truth is that in order to work, non-fiction requires the same creative writing skills as those of fiction. It needs a solid structure, a compelling narrative voice and a clear connection of ideas. The 'truth' of your work will not necessarily be what engages your readers, it will be how well you present that truth.

WHY BECOME A NON-FICTION WRITER?

Everyone tells real-life stories. Everyone comes home from even the simplest journey with an anecdote to tell. Something that happened to them or something they saw; a funny story told to them in a shop, or at work. We are a storytelling species. It is how we make sense of the world around us. For most people these stories are true. Real things that happened to real people in real places. Nevertheless everyone – often without realizing it – crafts their story. Shapes it so that it becomes more entertaining for the listener. In this way everyone already has the basics for producing great non-fiction work instinctively. Some people will be better at it than others, just as some people are naturally faster than others, but we all have the basic tools and can develop this native ability.

Everyone has had important, dramatic, surprising things happen to them. Equally, every family history is filled with characters and dramas: little legends that demand telling. And the broad sweep of history too, features people who have been forgotten and neglected. People whose stories deserve retelling for new audiences. As the writer of these stories, whether your own or other people's, you will gradually become an expert in some area of life. Your area of expertise might be narrow, but nevertheless part of the appeal of becoming a writer of non-fiction is that you will be the authority on the stories you choose to tell.

Finding a subject

You perhaps already have an idea of the story you want to write. Perhaps you lived through an era or in a place others know little about. Or you just want to get your life down so that others in your family – children or grandchildren for example – understand what those times were like for you. Whatever the reason, you are probably excited by the idea of writing an autobiography.

It might be that there are family legends, tales passed down from your own parents and other older relatives, that you want to verify.

There might be family characters whose lives seem worth exploring in more detail: a great-great uncle in the Royal Flying Corps, a great-great aunt who was one of the original suffragettes. An ancestor who sailed to America in search of a better life or who was fleeing persecution or economic hardship. One person who attended a writing course at the Ted Hughes Arvon Centre wanted to tell the story of her great-grandmother, the original inspiration for the Alice in Wonderland stories. Another was inspired by finding his grandfather's wartime diaries that recorded his time as a Battle of Britain fighter pilot.

Other writers have ambitions that are slightly larger in scope. One who came to our writing centre wanted to tell the story of a World War I poet, a contemporary of Owen and Sassoon, who she felt had been unjustly ignored and about whom little seemed to be known. Other people are excited by the idea of travel and reflecting on their travels for themselves and for others.

This is a similar exercise to one that we did in Chapter 2, 'Ideas and inspirations', but it is a variation that might help show you the huge range of creative avenues open to you.

Exercise 29

Make a simple timeline of all the key moments in your life. You might begin with the most obvious: your birth.

You might end up with something like this:

Nicola Lawson

Born 1968 Watford
Began at Bash Street Infants, Watford September 1973
Moved to Nigeria for Dad's work August 1976
Returned to Watford July 1981, attended Enid Blyton High School
1984 Parents divorced, moved to Colchester

Met Danny Finch who became first boyfriend, beginning of
   Wild Years
June 1986 Dropped out of High School, left home
June 1988 Married Guy Peters
September 1989 First child Tamara born
September 1992 Divorced Guy Peters, attended access course at
   local college
October 1994 Enrolled at Greenwich University
June 1997 Graduated with first class honours in History
September 1997 Got job with Greenwich museum service
Attended evening classes in life-drawing where met Barry Rogerson
August 1999 Married Barry Rogerson
July 2001 Second child Elliot born
October 2003 Moved to Spain with Barry to run a bar
February 2005 Returned to England to look after mother
   who was seriously ill
February 2006 Sold bar, returned to England. At Luton airport
   daughter Tamara spotted by modelling agent and given contract
   one month later
February 2007 Picked up copy of Vogue with Tamara on the front
   cover. Decide to write book about year as mother of aspiring model.

There's a lot here. And a lot that a reader could be interested in.
For example what exactly did Nicola do in her 'Wild Years'?
Why did her parents divorce? Why did her mother move from
Watford to Colchester after the divorce? What was life like for
a child spending a large part of her childhood in Nigeria? What
prompted Nicola to return to education? Why did her own first
marriage fail? What was Guy Peters like? What attracted her
to Barry Rogerson? Was he another student on the course? The
teacher? The model? What was life like in Spain as a bar owner
who was also trying to bring up a toddler? Why did she give up
work at the museum? Did she take her children with her when
she went back to look after her mum? Did her mother recover
and what was wrong with her anyway?

And then there are the big questions posed by the facts towards the
end of Nicola's timeline: how did the modelling agent approach

her daughter? What was Nicola's reaction? Was she suspicious? Delighted? And what were the stresses and strains of being plunged into that world? How did their lives change? How did Tamara cope with it all? What does Nicola feel about the modelling industry? Did she meet any interesting people? What does the future hold for the family now?

I have no doubt that your own timeline will be at least as interesting as this one and throw up as many questions and provide as many possibilities for future work.

What is clear though, is that if Nicola was telling her life story she probably wouldn't want to start right at the beginning. She herself made the decision that the most interesting thing for her to write about was the whole experience of becoming the mother of a young model.

She took an incident that happened late on in her timeline and took that as the subject of her first book. If she does it well that first book will be a mixture of memoir, a study of the fashion and modelling industries, and a biography of her daughter's short life. If she pulls it off it'll be a thought-provoking, entertaining read.

There were other avenues she could have gone down of course. Especially as I happen to know that her mother was the niece of the writer Georgina Basket, who produced popular detective novels in the 1940s. The same Georgina Basket who, family legend has it, was rumoured to have been a spy during World War II and dropped by parachute several times into occupied France in order to pass important messages to the Resistance.

She could also have written about the area of Spain where she and her second husband ran a bar. They lived in a small town, high in the Pyrenees, where Barry and Nicola and their children were the only English people and as such were objects of much curiosity. Fitting into the local community was often a challenge, particularly as they didn't speak the language and Barry never saw a reason to.

Ultimately, however, the experience was rewarding despite all the difficult and comical moments along the way. Nicola, Barry and the children were sad to leave and one of the first things Tamara did when she became a successful model was to buy a cottage in the town.

She could also have written about her experience of getting divorced from Guy Peters, which was astonishingly amicable and, she feels, could easily be a template for others going through similarly awkward situations. Perhaps her next book will be a manual for a civilized divorce.

Or she could have written about the eminent Victorian explorer and philanthropist, Lady Freeborn of Whittlesea, whose letters she came across while studying for her dissertation at Greenwich University and whom she has always wanted to research. Any moderately active life will furnish similar possibilities.

Structure

Insight

Possibly the most important thing about any piece of writing is the opening and this is just as true for a piece of non-fiction writing as it is for a novel.

The most obvious structure for a memoir or a biography is that suggested by William Shakespeare at the beginning of *As You Like It*. You must know it. It's the 'Seven Ages of Man' sonnet that begins with 'All the world's a Stage/And all the men and women merely players'.

Shakespeare's Seven Ages begins with the infant 'mewling and puking in the nurse's arms' and moves on through the schoolboy, the lover, the soldier, the justice, and the lean and slippered pantaloon, before the seventh age of second childishness sans teeth, sans eyes, sans everything.

It is easy to imagine the memoirist or the biographer looking back from the point of view of the sixth or even seventh age, and beginning their recollections with all that mewling and puking before moving on steadily through the other ages. And it might easily be quite dull. In any case, is the birth of the subject even the start of his story? In the novel *Tristram Shandy* the narrator finds himself compelled to begin his life story from the moment of his conception, which means he has to describe the childhood of his parents and so on. The story hardly gets started. A modern reader wants to be pulled into the story straightaway. Here's an exercise that might help give an insight into how you might shape your non-fiction work.

CREATE A TIMELINE

Exercise 30

Think of all the things you did yesterday. Make a list, starting with getting up and ending with going to bed. Now choose the most interesting thing that happened yesterday and write that down in as much detail as you can. I guarantee that at least one interesting thing happened yesterday. Try and capture it all. Describe the characters involved and where they were. Just stick to the who, the what, the where and the why. Keep it short.

Now complete this next exercise which focuses on one area of the timeline.

Exercise 31

Go back to your timeline and pick a pivotal moment in your life. One incident that seemed to sum up where your

(Contd)

life was going. It might be a row with a parent. A proposal of marriage. A stag or hen night. A job interview. The birth of a child. The arrival in a foreign country. It can be large or small, the important thing is that it is one vivid episode which has stayed with you for many years. Write it up as if you were telling it for the first time to an interested person who doesn't know you or anything about the people involved. Write it in the present tense as though the event is happening right now. Begin with the words 'I am...' and carry on from there. Again, keep it reasonably short, no more than 250 words. Try and set the scene; make the readers really feel like they are witnesses.

Example:

I am sitting in my father's chair. The leather armchair with the odd high back. We are waiting for him to come home, my mother and I. I have something important to say.

The point is that your memoir or biography needn't necessarily begin at the beginning and move forward from there. That is, of course, one way to do it, but it might be an idea to start with something that reveals something about the character, or something that foreshadows the kind of person your subject became.

CONSIDER VARIOUS VIEWPOINTS

Here is another exercise designed to help you think about the structure of a piece of creative non-fiction.

Exercise 32

Imagine that it is your funeral. Make notes about who will be there and who might be missing. Now imagine that a good friend is standing up to deliver the eulogy. What might

they say about you? What stories might they tell, designed
to show your character in all its eccentric humanity?
(I already know that you are eccentric because you have
decided to become a creative writer!) Crucially, what
might they leave out in telling your story to the assembled
congregation?

Being selective is a skill of all writing and it is especially true of
non-fiction writing. What *not* to write is every bit as important
as deciding what to put in and where. At a funeral each speaker
has just a few minutes to deliver a monologue about the deceased,
so your eulogy to yourself will need to be just a few pages long
but has still to cover the most important facts of your life and to
tell a few good stories too. It's not easy is it? But it's possibly the
most useful exercise in structure there is and you may well find out
something about yourself as well.

If you find the idea of writing your own funeral address too
depressing you could try preparing a best man's speech for your
own wedding, or a father's speech if you are a bride. The problems
are still the same: what goes in, what stays out and what order do
you place the events in?

Of course the exercise above assumes that you will present yourself
in a reasonably good light. Best man speeches can be teasing or
risqué, but are usually affectionate. Funeral speeches are nearly
always respectful. It could be an interesting exercise to try it again
from the point of view of someone who doesn't like you much.
You might be one of those fortunate few who have managed to get
through life without making enemies, but that is not true for most
of us. Most of us have ex-wives, ex-lovers, ex-friends, ex-colleagues
who we know would not be all that flattering if they had the
chance to write down their true feelings about us. If writing is, as
Hemingway said it was, a case of writing 'hard about what hurts',
then we should try and put ourselves in the shoes of someone who
doesn't share our benign view of ourselves.

Exercise 33

Imagine that someone who you suspect doesn't like you much is writing you a letter about the way you have lived your life. What are they going to say? What will they put in that the funeral orator or best man might leave out? Make notes and then write the letter, trying to capture your former friend's way of speaking. Try and inhabit their mindset as much as possible.

The reason for doing this exercise is to reinforce the obvious point that there are always at least two sides to every story and it's your duty as a biographer or an autobiographer to acknowledge other points of view. However, don't allow the need for balance to cause you to lose focus – you don't want to confuse your readers, and it is absolutely OK to have a strong consistent argument.

Insight

No one is interested in just hearing about triumphs and successes or in simply learning about what a wonderful chap the person you are writing about is or was. They want the darker, harder truths too.

Flexibility

Lives are awkward, restless creatures. They simply won't stand still and they resist being encased into a rigid cage no matter how carefully we have designed it. As you research the life, place or period you have decided to write about you will find that your preconceptions are challenged all the time. Your research may well lead you off into places where you didn't expect to go. Those characters you thought might be heroes will turn out to be not quite as heroic as you had thought, the villains not quite so villainous. Happy childhoods may turn out to have been miserable all along. Your own past actions may not stand up to much close scrutiny.

It is in this gap between assumptions and realities that the real fun of being a creative non-fiction writer lies. It can be unsettling. But, like a good detective, you have to go wherever the evidence takes you. This means that your plan must be flexible, adaptable. You must be able to keep an open mind and to change it when necessary. It's no good being like the stubborn politician who thinks they are showing courage when they announce that they are not for turning, or that they have no reverse gear. A vehicle that can't turn round or backtrack when circumstances demand it, is more or less useless. And so is a biographer.

Exercise 34

Here is a little exercise in flexibility. Write down something that happened to you when you were a child. It doesn't need to be a big thing. It can be the day you fell off your bike. But when you've written down the facts as you know them, call up someone else in your family who might know a little about the incident. Read them what you've written and ask if they have anything to add. They almost certainly will. Now rewrite the incident including any new facts or details you have been given. In any piece of memoir writing or biography this kind of experience will occur frequently and it is best to accept new information gracefully and alter your plan, rather than trying to make it fit your established world-view.

Beginning your research

PERSONAL CONTACTS

With any kind of research-based project the best places to start are the most obvious. Begin with personal contacts. If it is an autobiography you are working on then your family and friends will be the first port of call. After this will come teachers, work colleagues, those who knew you as a teammate or a band member, etc. If it is a biography then tell everyone you know what you are working on. I can guarantee that nearly all of them will have contacts of their own, or suggestions of where you should go for information. Some of these – perhaps the majority – will not be relevant but many will be good ideas that will save you much valuable time. You may even find others who are working in a similar field and who have contacts and information that they are willing to share. Certainly, someone who has done something similar recently will have much useful advice to share. Someone who has, say, written a biography of their father who was a submariner during World War II, will have lots to say about how to go about finding the relevant records of your own great-grandfather if he was a sailor during World War I.

ONLINE SOURCES

Most people these days begin any research with the internet. And it is true that search engines have brought a staggering amount of research about almost anything within reach of everyone. And most of it's free too. The trouble is that a lot of it is rubbish.

There's no filter, no quality control. Anyone can say anything they like about anything at all and publish it as fact. Lunatics and fanatics, freaks and weirdos of every shape haunt the alleyways of the internet like a particularly ferocious breed of zombie in a horror flick. There's a lot of seductive nonsense out there and you'll need patience and a highly developed nose for nonsense to avoid being infected by it. Tread carefully and trust nothing on the web unless it comes from unimpeachable sources.

It is, however, getting better. Just as the Wild West was cleaned up as the banks and railroads moved into the lawless frontier towns, so the virtual cities of the web are becoming more orderly. Many of the major libraries – including those of most universities – now have a web presence and you can access their resources from your living room. Likewise, one of your major research tools – the *Dictionary of National Biography* – can be studied via the internet.

In the UK, census returns up to 1911 are also available on the internet now, as are lots of other government records. Churches too – which were for a long time the principal record keepers – have begun to place some of their records online.

Here is a list of some of the websites that you might find most useful in your research:

▶ *A2A – the Access to Archives project – www.a2a.org.uk*
  This contains catalogues of numerous archives in England and Wales.
▶ *SCAN – the Scottish Archives Network – www.scan.org.uk*
  This aims to provide a single electronic catalogue of the records held in more than 50 Scottish archives. SCAN also aims to make some documents, for example the wills and testaments of Scots from 1500 to 1875, available online.
▶ *NRA – the National Register of Archives – www.hmc.gov.uk.nra*
  The NRA is maintained by the Historical Manuscripts Commission and allows searches of a wide range of archives. It covers archive deposits across the UK as well as listing UK material in foreign archives.
▶ *The Church of the Latter Day Saints (Mormons) – www.familysearch.org*
  The Mormons place enormous emphasis on genealogy and so have launched a massive project to transcribe all the birth, death and marriage records from around the world.

The Church also maintains a number of Family History Centres providing facilities where researchers can study.

▶ *1911 Census (England and Wales) – www.1911census.co.uk/*
Lots of useful information for those researching the past.
Go to www.nationalarchives.gov.uk/records/census-records.htm
for information on censuses in England and Wales prior to
this date, and www.scotlandspeople.gov.uk/ for censuses in
Scotland.

LIBRARIES AND PUBLIC RECORDS OFFICES

I love libraries. Quiet places devoted to study and to reading that are free and open to everyone. There is no better index to how civilized a society has become than in the way it funds and values its libraries. My stepson's school recently did away with the notion of a library. They decided it wasn't cool, that kids were put off using it because of its intimidating name. They renamed the space the LRC – short for Learning Resource Centre. Which prompted my cynical response that maybe we should rename books themselves. Maybe we should call them HLDs – Handheld Learning Devices. This kind of Newspeak is a nonsense of course. A library *is* a learning resource centre. That's what the word means and so now, in its ridiculous efforts to be 'with it' and 'trendy', the school uses three words instead of one. The place itself hasn't changed. It's still a roomful of books plus some computers. And nearly all libraries are fitted out with PCs now. There's nothing special about that.

But the best thing about libraries are librarians. Librarians are generally hugely knowledgeable about all manner of subjects, and making friends with the librarian at the one nearest you will save you an enormous amount of time. Remember, every query that you have, big or small, is almost certainly one that they'll have heard and dealt with already. The same is true of public records offices. There is nothing like being led gently through a maze of ancient documentation by someone who knows all the pathways and safe routes out.

Useful tools

Here are some of the most typical forms of material that you will find in a local archive or library that might be most helpful to you:

▶ *Voters' rolls or register of electors*
  These provide evidence for residence and evidence of social–economic status. Remember that women didn't get the vote until 1918 (and then it was only for those over 30) and it wasn't until 1928 that they gained full equality with men (votes for all at age 21). Single women got the vote in municipal elections in 1869. Franchise was also restricted for men prior to 1867.
▶ *Valuation rolls*
  Very useful for establishing property ownership and, from this, for deducing the social status of an occupant.
▶ *School records*
  School logbooks can reveal a great deal about life outside the classroom, the impact of local epidemics being just one example. More obviously, admission registers, reports and school logbooks can provide specific information about this crucial aspect of your subject's childhood development.
▶ *Welfare records*
  Included in these records might be the records and logs of workhouses and other forms of relief paid to those who were destitute or unable, through illness or old age, to provide for themselves or their families.
▶ *Local authority records*
  These might include the minutes of local authority meetings, as well as documents relating to local planning, health,

*welfare, education, streets, shops, pavements, etc. Local
authorities also maintained the burgess rolls which are very
valuable documents for discovering information on people
during times of very limited franchise. (Burgesses are, broadly,
heads of households with property and a trade, and therefore
often had the right to vote.)*

▶ *Church records*
*These include information not only on births, marriages and
deaths but also on education and welfare. In addition many
people were employed by the church, and records and accounts
can provide valuable information about life in the parish.*

▶ *Local newspapers*
*Libraries may well have complete back issues of newspapers
(including many which no longer exist) and you may find
your subject appearing in the pages of their local paper,
either in news reports, in the letters columns or as the
subject of an obituary.*

▶ *Local directories*
*These usually consist of an alphabetical listing of property
owners and tenants and quite often give the occupations of
the householders too. In addition to this information they
frequently give details on justices of the peace, local societies
and charities, and voluntary bodies.*

There is a lot more than this to be found in libraries but the above
should give you some sense of how important it is for the creative
non-fiction writer to know their way around these places.

Organizing your material

The temptation when you are relying on research is to stick in
everything you know about a subject. You will have discovered
amazing facts, and a lot of them, and it is natural to want to give
as complete a picture as possible. That is, however, not your job.
Your job is to make the subject come alive and you can't do that
by including everything. You have got to tell a story and to do

that you have to work on shaping your material. Just as a sculptor discards most of the clay or bronze he is working with, so much of your information is not going to make it into the main body of your book. The key is to read, summarize and select.

Insight

Reading documents in full before summarizing will ensure that key facts stay in your mind. If you simply photocopy and file you might well find that you are simply carting huge bundles of files from home to library and back again without ever really coming to grips with them.

Tip

When writing up your notes, don't be afraid of quoting directly from legal documents. The wording, however archaic, will often add authenticity and liveliness to your piece.

Keeping it legal

There are three basic things to be aware of in keeping a non-fiction book on the right side of the law:

1 *copyright*
2 *permissions*
3 *acknowledgements*.

Copyright exists to protect authors from having their work stolen. If you quote short extracts – a line or two – for educational purposes, then this is usually alright. If you want to quote longer chunks of another writer's work then you will need to get the permission of the copyright holder and there will usually be a fee involved in this. If the writer is dead, copyright on their works will be held by their estate and is usually retained for 70 years after their death. (There are exceptions, and different laws apply in different countries, so do check.)

Copyright exists on letters and legal documents as well as on books and published material, so you will have to gain permission from the owners of these rights too if you wish to quote from them. It is the writer of the letter who owns the copyright **NOT** the receiver. So even if you are the recipient of a hundred letters from a great-aunt vividly detailing her experiences as a spy in World War II you can't publish extracts from them without express permission – and get it in writing – from her or her estate.

Official documents such as birth and marriage certificates are also subject to copyright and this is generally owned by the Crown or the Local Authorities. Again, permission must be sought – and usually paid for – before publication.

Copyright can be a fraught, vexing and tiresome business but it is absolutely essential that you make sure you are covered. It should also go without saying that all material you use should be acknowledged. All sources should be properly credited from the books you have used, all the way to that ten-minute interview you did with Uncle Herb in his retirement home on the Costa Brava.

Writing a proposal

We'll cover more about getting books published in a later chapter, but there are some clear differences between the paths to publication for non-fiction books and for novels and poetry collections that are worth dealing with here.

Unlike novels, non-fiction books are usually sold to publishers on the basis of a proposal and a sample chapter. Most agents and publishers are not – at an early stage with an untried author – going to read a whole manuscript. You need to put together a persuasive proposal. This proposal needs to be short and punchy. But it needs to get across some important information. It needs to tell the editor what your qualifications are for telling this story. So any expertise or experience that you have needs to be flagged up.

It also needs to give the publishers or agents some idea of the potential market for the book.

Editors are, quite rightly, interested in projects that will make them money and you need to be aware of this too. You'll need to indicate what other books on this subject exist and what your book will add. If no books exist then that is worth pointing out too. Explain clearly who or what the subject of the book is and why he, she or it is worth writing about.

Insight

Spend some real time on your proposal. It needs to give the flavour of the piece, so your distinctive voice needs to come over clearly. You are aiming to intrigue and excite, so style is important. The storytelling skills of a non-fiction writer are important. You know that the story you have to tell is fascinating and alive; it demands to be heard. You must communicate that passion to an editor in your sample chapter.

Submitting will be covered in more detail in Chapter 19, but just in case you rush ahead without reading the rest of the book: remember that your text should be neatly and correctly printed out, double-spaced on one side and not bound or stapled. Do remember to number your pages and have your contact details on your covering letter. You'll find out more about covering letters later on too.

Exercise 35

Write a two-page proposal for a non-fiction subject that you think might interest an editor. It can be for an autobiography, a biography or any other subject. Remember, your aim is simply to intrigue your reader enough that they ask to see more of your work.

This has been a fairly long chapter, but it's a growing area of interest among writers, readers and publishers. I'd like to finish with an exercise adapted from one given to me by the biographers Carole Angier and Sally Cline who, between them, have written ten major biographies including those on Zelda Fitzgerald, Primo Levi and Radclyffe Hall.

Exercise 36

You'll need a partner for this.

1 *Interview a friend or a family member (or, even better, another writer) about an event or a relationship in their past. Keep it short; 15 minutes should be plenty of time if you can keep them focused.*
2 *Write a biographical piece based on the interview. Take no more than 30 minutes to write the piece.*
3 *Ask your subject to comment on the piece.*

The above exercise is very good for showing the differences between biographical and autobiographical writing. It is also very good for showing how much you can accomplish in a short amount of time. It's actually quite a sophisticated exercise, so if it doesn't work out the first time, find a new subject and try it again. It's a particularly good one to try with someone else who wants to write because then you can experience what it is like to be the interviewee. This is an extremely useful thing to have done when you come to interview people for real.

Professional tip from Ian Marchant

If someone came to me saying, 'I've a great idea for a non-fiction book' I'd say, 'Excellent, but the idea has to be the easy bit so think of another two good ideas before you over-commit to the first one.' Ideas can't be copyrighted; they are just out there. Sometimes what might seem like a great idea for you might well have occurred to at least one other writer. Keep the ideas coming. Write a 200-word summation of the three ideas, then chew on 'em for a bit. Only when you're really happy with your original idea, and have weighed it against other possibilities, should you begin to write your book proposal.

And, I'd also like to tell this anecdote: I once took an idea for a radio travel programme to the BBC. The producer listened to my idea and then said, 'Why you and not someone famous?' I didn't have an answer at the time, but now I know that the ideas I pitch could only be done by me. Make sure that your book can only be written by you.'

Ian Marchant is the author of the memoirs *The Longest Crawl* and *Parallel Lines* (both Bloomsbury).

10 THINGS TO REMEMBER

1 *Everyone has had important, dramatic, surprising things happen to them.*

2 *Start with the living before moving on to the dead. Those closest to you may have important things to say that could help your project.*

3 *Non-fiction writers are first and foremost telling a story. Focus on what's interesting more than what's true.*

4 *Give us the dark as well as the light. The rain as well as the sunshine. And vice versa.*

5 *Be prepared to change your mind about your subject.*

6 *Make friends with librarians and archivists.*

7 *Keep it legal. Take advice if you have to.*

8 *Remember that people have a right to privacy.*

9 *Spend as much time on your proposal as you do on any part of your book.*

10 *Don't start with a birth. Find a way into your story that is full of action and incident.*

7

Travel writing

In this chapter you will learn:

- *the importance of paying attention to your surroundings*
- *to make the familiar exotic*
- *what readers want from travel writing*
- *to put yourself in the picture.*

> *Like all great travellers, I have seen more than I remember,
> and remember more than I have seen.*
>
> Benjamin Disraeli

Stand and stare

The one necessity of any kind of writing is to pay attention to what is going on around you. Most people are too caught up in the business of living to take the time to properly stand and stare. In most walks of life simply watching the world go by is frowned upon. Do too much of it and it can get you fired or divorced. We live in a time when people are expected to have full diaries: to juggle work, family and relationships around a tight and full schedule. Every unforgiving minute should be used to the full. Squeezed for every second of potential.

But for the creative artist, and for the writer especially, taking the time and trouble to simply observe what's going on around us is actually the entire point of our work. The job of the writer is to make the strange comprehensible. And also, of course, to make whatever is familiar new and strange. If most people don't have time amid the hurly-burly of life to make sense of it, then the writer has to do it for them. We stand and stare so that others don't have to. And by our example perhaps those too caught up in the frenetic business of twenty-first century life will start to learn to live at a more sustainable pace. Perhaps they too will discover the joys of simply looking and thinking.

The travel writer in particular needs the ability to look hard at the everyday. Readers of travel articles and books are looking for the writer to give them a flavour of the spirit of a place, and, paradoxical as it might seem, you can only do this by writing in detail about it. You can't resort to waffle. If your readers are thinking that one day they too might want to go to the same place, then you will need to give them practical tips to help them find their way around, facts about the country to enable them to travel safely and with as little inconvenience as possible. Travellers have a time budget as well as a financial one and so will need enough information to enable them to spend time as well as cash wisely.

Putting personality into the picture

It is, however, likely that most of your readers will not necessarily be looking to visit any time soon. They are visiting vicariously via your words. And for these readers you will need to provide authentic sensual detail. And, of course, all readers are going to want more than just the facts, however colourful. They are going to want to feel that they are in the company of a stimulating personality. They will want to trust their guide to impart knowledge but they will also want to spend time with someone of warmth and good humour. It is just as important with this kind of writing that your personal voice comes across, that your engagement with the culture you are describing is obvious.

The following exercises were given to me by the writer Miranda France, whose book about Spain, *Don Quixote's Delusions: Travels in Castilian Spain,* is an intoxicating mixture of reportage, history, memoir and literary criticism. They seem to me excellent for helping to develop the skills necessary for bringing an unknown place alive for readers.

Exercise 37

A still life: think of an object in your home that would seem mundane to an outsider but is precious to you. In two paragraphs, try to describe the object, then unfold a story behind it.

Exercise 38

Sense of place: dredge up the memory of a place you have been to. It could be somewhere you knew well and went to every day, or somewhere you have been to just once, say last night. Think about the smell, the sound of the place. If it was a chip shop, was the Formica sticky? What was on the radio? Was the smell agreeable or acrid? What were people talking about at the next table?

Exercise 39

A desire: write about a person or a thing that you yearn for – it could be the love of your life or a cream cake. Make it deeply personal and poignant or utterly trivial and comic. Or mix all of these elements.

Remember that all the best travel writers, from Daniel Defoe and Samuel Johnson in the eighteenth century through to the best modern travel writers such as Bill Bryson, Ian Marchant and Miranda herself, have all given a lot of themselves in their writing. It is the mixture of their acute and accurate observations and a very personal style, plus the way that they drip-feed their own histories that makes their take on places so appealing.

Insight

In order to write an interesting travel piece you don't need to go to exotic locations, you simply need the ability to look at the world in a new way and that means that you need to spend time just paying close attention to what happens around you all the time, wherever you happen to be.

Exercise 40

Write a piece about your home town or village designed to intrigue anyone who might not have visited it before. Try and make it as personal as you can but don't use more than 300 words.

Inevitably, some of you will live in beautiful places and others in areas considered drab by outsiders. I'd be willing to bet that pieces produced by those living in the less obviously attractive places are every bit as fascinating as pieces coming from those who live in beauty spots. All good writing is about people, in the final analysis. And people, wherever they live, are endlessly fascinating.

Professional tip from Christopher George

Take boring notes. Menu prices, hotel tariffs, bus timetables, etc. There's no point describing a shikara's wake of burnished gold in the sunset-surface of Nageen lake unless you can also tell me how much it costs to hire one. Evoke and inform, that's the mantra ... inform and evoke.

Christopher George is the author of *Towards the Sun* (Hodder Murray).

5 THINGS TO REMEMBER

1 *Take time to stand and stare.*

2 *Put your own personality into any travel piece.*

3 *Remember that what is close to home may be as interesting as the exotic.*

4 *Imagine why a reader might want to know about a particular place.*

5 *Evoke and inform.*

8

Blogging

In this chapter you will learn:
- *what makes a successful blog*
- *the uses of blogging*
- *how to stand out in the blogocracy*
- *about the dangers of blogging.*

Any sufficiently advanced technology is indistinguishable from magic.

Arthur C. Clarke

The magic of blogging

Blogging is a new medium for your writing. It is a way of reaching millions, possibly billions, of people with your thoughts and opinions. It is a public forum for discussion largely uncontrolled by governments, business and other self-appointed guardians of free speech. It is, or can be, a place where your voice can have as much weight as the most highly regarded writer.

You need no permission or commission to speak your mind. And you don't even have to expose yourself. You can do it anonymously. You can write about anything: from how delightful your grandchildren are, to the evil of your own government's foreign policy – sometimes within the same piece. You can post photos and music and videos. It is, in theory at least, a return to the ferment of ideas that flourished in Europe just after the invention of the printing press. It is a defiantly democratic medium which has the potential to empower ordinary people to express themselves without the filter of the traditional printed media with their phalanxes of editors standing between them and an audience. It is a hugely powerful tool for building grassroots social movements, allowing activists to communicate their ideas directly to the people. On the other hand it is also an opportunity for every eccentric with access to a laptop to pollute hyperspace with drivel of the most pernicious kind.

The word 'blog' derives from web-log and essentially means a diary. But, unlike the traditional diary where the writer keeps a secret record of their daily life, thoughts or feelings, the blogger makes the journal available to everyone.

Of course the identity of the blogger may be secret – most people write under a pseudonym – but their activities and thoughts are very public. Blogging has had a powerful effect on the media life of this country. It has revolutionized the process of commenting on events. Via a blogging site anyone at all can have their say about almost anything. It is a valuable democratic tool and allows us insight into areas of life to which in past decades only the privileged few had access.

WHO BLOGS?

Policemen blog. Nurses blog. Teachers blog. Doctors blog. MPs blog. Prostitutes blog. People under siege in war zones blog. So do the soldiers doing the besieging. Thanks to blogging sites such as www.blogspot.com (still the biggest but there are plenty of others where you can set up a free blogging account) we have access to the thoughts of millions of ordinary people living all over the world. As a reader of blogs you can read and respond to the daily record of life in all parts of the world and under all conditions.

Some of these blogs have become very famous. Belle de Jour is the pseudonym of a high-class call girl who writes a blog which became a very successful book and then a television drama in the UK starring Billie Piper. Newspapers scour the blogs to find out what ordinary people think about the news and adapt their content to suit. Meanwhile publishers are always looking for a blog that might make a saleable book.

WHY BLOG?

Part of the answer is contained in the paragraphs above. Blogging is a chance to say what you feel about current events, big and small. It is a chance to get your writing read by a global audience. It can even be a route to publication for a lucky, particularly interesting few. But its best benefits for an aspiring writer are that it encourages a habit of daily reflection.

Most writing teachers have always encouraged new writers to keep a diary as it helps your style enormously to keep a coherent record of your life. It is invaluable practice in ordering your thoughts. And of course, it is a record of events which you can work on later and hone into more polished pieces. A diary can build up into a treasure chest of future material.

Blogging is similar, with the added benefit that people can comment on your writing. They can, of course, comment unfavourably. And, more seriously, you might find other writers using your material. I know several professional writers who trawl blogs looking for inside info on occupations and lifestyles that might help with whatever they are writing about.

How to stand out from the crowd

If you have gone to the trouble of posting your thoughts up on the web, then you probably want at least a few readers. Yet with so many blogs, and with so few of any merit, why should readers wade through the many screen miles of turgid and self-regarding prose to discover your site?

The first thing is to make sure that what you have to say is going to be of real interest. It is time, therefore, to evaluate your life in terms of what might intrigue other people. Unlikely contrasts are always a good source of interest. Are you a middle-class, southern woman living on a big northern council estate? Are you a man doing what is usually considered to be a woman's job? Are you an older person sharing a university apartment with students many years younger than yourself? Do you have 11 children? Did you become a grandparent in your thirties? Do you live in an unusual place in an unusual set up: a commune for example, or a kibbutz? Did you quit a high-flying job to become a speech therapist?

SURPRISING TRUTHS

A game that is quite often played by those trying to bond groups of disparate individuals together is to get each member of the group to tell the others something about themselves that they think will surprise all the others. When playing this game I've had confessions ranging from the innocuous 'I've always wanted to run a pub', to the shyly boastful 'My band once appeared on *Top of the Pops*', to the compelling – if scary – 'I could kill you all with my bare hands'. (This last confession came from a mild-mannered lady on a children's writing course who, it turned out, had once been an officer in the British special forces.)

If you are going to blog, it makes sense to play this game on your own. What is there about your life that will surprise and intrigue the world? There is bound to be something. This is your chance to review what there is about your life that would be of immediate interest to a stranger.

When you have decided then focus on that one thing. Try not to make your blog a sprawling repository of your thoughts and feelings on every subject. The key difference between a blog and a traditional diary is that you are writing for an audience.

You must engage your readers, keep them interested so that they don't click to another part of the web. It's a hard trick to pull off.

People browsing the web are like particularly restless jackdaws, forever wondering if there is a shinier nugget somewhere else in hyperspace.

Insight

With the limited attention span of the web audience in mind, adhere firmly to the 'less is more' principle. Try to ration yourself to writing about just one thing that happens to you every day, or every week.

Some health warnings

Material you want to place on the web should be handled as though it were radioactive. After all, it might well lie there quietly polluting the future for longer than a piece of discarded uranium. Your thoughts, photos, videos, jokes and careless libels may be on the net forever, as incorruptible as disposable nappies in a landfill. And more public, and more toxic! There are numerous talented potential leaders in all fields of human endeavour whose achievements will be curtailed by a stupid set of photos taken at a drunken student party and then posted on the internet, to be resurrected at the most cruelly inconvenient of moments.

It won't just be photos that cause trouble. If you write about your boss in terms that identify them then you could soon be looking for a new job.

One drawback of blogging is that people can very quickly become victims of their own success. Write a good one and word of mouth may quickly bring you a surprising number of regular readers, among whom may be people who think they know who you are. Some of them may be right.

The most famous diarist of them all was Samuel Pepys. His journals, written in shorthand, lay unread in a Cambridge University library for 150 years before being translated and published (and even then they were heavily edited). Imagine if Pepys had written a blog (maybe it would be www.confessionsofanavyofficeclerk.blogspot.com), his accounts of life in London would surely have garnered an audience very quickly. A junior civil servant nudges his mate in some open plan office somewhere in Cheapside. The mate gets on to his girlfriend who works on a glossy lifestyle magazine. She writes a little piece about the racy double life led by public officials these days.

Pretty soon King Charles II is clicking on what we used to call the information superhighway to find a lavish description of Nell Gwynn's décolletage. He is not amused. And thus, one promising career in public service is ruined: Britain never gets her Navy sorted, and 100 years later the French win the Napoleonic Wars.

This might seem extreme but the point is that words on the net may come back to haunt you when you least expect it.

Exercise 41

Think about what you've done so far today. Select just one incident and write about that. If you can bring to your description some special insight into a part of your life which others don't know about, that will add something. Try and do this for the next week and show the results to a trusted friend (TF). If the TF likes what you've written and thinks both that it adds to the sum of human knowledge and won't get you (or anyone else you mentioned in it) into terrible trouble in the foreseeable future, then – and only then – consider posting your blog.

Professional tip from Caroline Smailes

I think that the key to blogging is the interactive element, being prepared to visit and comment and respond to comments given to you. Developing and being accepted into networks requires effort, like any developing friendship. Content and style varies and is a matter of personal taste. For me, the blogs that I enjoy have an honesty, a social interaction, a persona that is interesting and accessible.

Caroline Smailes' blog can be found at www.carolinesmailes.co.uk. Her novel *In Search of Adam* (The Friday Project) was published after she wrote about it on the web.

TOP 10 BLOGS FOR WRITERS

- *Me and My Big Mouth*
  meandmybigmouth.typepad.com

- *Writer Unboxed*
  www.writerunboxed.com

- *Copyblogger*
  www.copyblogger.com

- *Men with Pens*
  menwithpens.ca

- *Freelance Writing Jobs*
  www.freelancewritinggigs.com

- *The Urban Muse*
  www.urbanmusewriter.com

- *Remarkable Communication*
  www.remarkable-communication.com

- *Confident Writing*
  confidentwriting.com

- *Women on Writing*
  www.wow-womenonwriting.com/blog.html

- *Always Have a Notebook*
  thesecondbesttime.blogspot.com

9

Writing for children

In this chapter you will learn:
- *the importance of children's writing*
- *what age group to write for*
- *the necessity of honesty and the joy of being rude*
- *how to deal with problems.*

> *Oh, grown-ups cannot understand*
> *And grown-ups never will,*
> *How short's the way to fairy land*
> *Across the purple hill.*

Alfred Noyes

The rarest kind of 'best'

Our children deserve the best and that is as true for writing as it is for anything else. We live in a culture of plenty. There is, for most people in the UK, plenty of food, decent accommodation, as well as education, health, recreation and entertainment facilities that would astonish our recent ancestors. Everyone in the UK is already a lotto winner when compared with the majority of the world's population. And yet we often seem determined to squander these gifts. Many of our children are bored witless despite a plethora of entertainment choices that someone born even just a generation back can only marvel at. I was born in the 1960s and who then could have predicted digital television, never mind the rise of the internet games where hundreds of thousands of players compete without ever meeting – without even being on the same continent? Wii, PSP, Nintendo DS, giant plasma screen High Definition televisions and computer games to suit every taste and yet... and yet... many children seem restless, dissatisfied and parents are consequently frustrated and cross.

The trouble is that a lot of the entertainment choices pushed at children are junk. The equivalent of a non-stop diet of fizzy pop and sweets. Children need wholesome stories the way that they need fibre and fruit. There has been a concerted effort to reintroduce children to the benefits of exercise and decent nutrition and similarly, with less media fanfare, many parents, publishers, librarians and teachers have been fighting a battle to engage children with the joy of reading. To show them that life needn't be lived through a lens.

Reading might seem hard work when compared with sitting in front of the television all day. And every normal parent has used children's television as a babysitter from time to time. And yes, television and computers can be educational, but so can dissection and we don't usually allow children to undertake that kind of experiment unsupervised.

The main drawback to allowing children unfettered access to the various screen-based entertainments is that the lassitude it induces becomes addictive. Did you know that watching television uses less energy than sleeping? But even worse than this, is the fact that a room without someone burbling away in the corner begins to seem unnatural to children. They become unnerved by quiet and by reflection because it is so rare to them. They become scared of it, the way that previous generations were scared of woods and the dark.

What is the real thing?

We all of us know this. A book is the real thing for a child when it demands to be read over and over. A story is the real thing when we know every word by heart and still we want it read to us. A book is the real thing when it completely absorbs the child. Crucially it also needs to engage adults. For younger children a big part of the enjoyment of being read to is spending time on a shared activity with a grown-up. If it is clear that the grown-up in question is bored and would rather be doing something else, then the child will be anxious, distressed and restless too.

Children are a difficult audience. Not only are there all the competing entertainments, in what has become a visual rather than a literary culture, but children are very opinionated about the books that they do like. Generally kids like books that are funny, that are full of adventure, that feature strong, close relationships, that are gripping without being too frightening and that end more or less happily. It's a tall order but on the plus side, if a child loves your book then they will love it forever, read it over and over, and seek out other stories that you may write. Children are a loyal and passionate audience as well as a demanding one. They are honest too.

Insight

If a little girl says she loves your book then you know that she's not just being nice, she really does love it. If a lad says your book is 'well ace' then you have a real fan. Adults will say things just to be nice. Kids, however polite, will give it to you straight.

We once had a poet teach a course at the writing centre, who asked a group of Liverpool schoolchildren what they thought of the poem he had just read them. There was a half-second pause before a girl piped up, 'I thought it were rubbish. Really borin'', whereupon the poet took offence. Thankfully the opposite story is more usual where children meet an author and find that they are pleasantly surprised by how enthralled they have become just by having someone read something to them. The thrill of being gradually drawn into a story can appear like a kind of low-key miracle to many of today's children.

Deciding on an age group

This is your first challenge when writing for children but it is worth thinking about right at the beginning. What is also worth getting right early on is how children at a particular age think and speak. An eight-year-old today may well not talk or even think like an eight-year-old did in 1972. In truth, the fundamentals probably haven't changed all that much, but the language and culture that surrounds today's eight-year-old is very different. It obviously helps if you know some children!

Whatever age you decide to write for the crucial thing is not to patronize or talk down to your audience. Children want to be talked to on the level. As a schoolteacher for several years I quickly discovered that in conversation with a child it was always best to assume that they were a little older, a little more well-read and a little more articulate than they actually were.

Insight
Children like to be thought of as grown up and will rise to the occasion if treated in this way. It's no different with books. Write plainly and simply, but don't write childishly.

Exercise 42

When you next visit a bookshop, spend some time in the children's section. Take notice of how the books are arranged. Generally publishers will want to put your book into a category immediately. Is it a baby book? Is it for pre-school age? A picture book for children between five and seven years old? Or is it a core fiction, i.e. for 7–12-year-olds? After this you are into 'writing for young adults'. Spend some serious time browsing and reading, rediscovering your own preferences. What are you most drawn to?

If you are uncertain where your own style might fit, try writing a paragraph or two of a story for each age group. Have some books to hand to help with vocabulary and style.

Exercise 43

Spend time with some children. Get them to bring you their favourite books. Read to them, or get them to read to you if they're old enough. Play some games with them, but remember to let them take the lead. The children will be delighted. It's no easy task for even the most winning child to get an adult's close attention. It helps if you've got your own to hand, but grandchildren, nieces, nephews, the kids next door or those at a local school will also appreciate you taking an interest. (Do please remember to get proper permissions though! If you're going into a school you'll need a Criminal Records Bureau check which the school can arrange.)

Losing past loves

One of the great things about writing for children is that the books young people fall in love with stay a treasured memory forever. Like childhood itself, a book can often seem even better when seen through the enchanted specs of memory. You will have you own favourites. The Famous Five, The Fantastic Four, Just William, Swallows and Amazons, Molesworth, Biggles, Tracey Beaker, Narnia, The Borrowers and Harry Potter; there's a good chance that you may well have been passionately attached to some of these characters. Well, now you need to let them go. Remember what you liked about them certainly, but don't think that they will come to your aid now. The world is a very different place and children, being infinitely adaptable, are wired for the one they find themselves in.

Exercise 44

Try and find a passage in a classic children's book that you particularly enjoy and rewrite it in a style that a modern child might appreciate, updating the language and setting as you see fit. Be careful. It's harder than you think to update an acknowledged classic and still make it inspiring and rich.

Originality

Having an original idea that has the legs to sustain an entire book is perhaps the hardest thing in all writing. You might find yourself coming close to despair. All the best ideas for children's fiction can seem like they're already taken. In particular, stories involving toys that come to life, animals with human characteristics and trainee wizards all seem to have been done to death. Nevertheless, themes for children's books are universal and timeless – the secret world, the magical journey, unexpected dangers, being lost, gaining new powers – and original ways of treating these themes are all around you just waiting to be discovered.

In essence all children's stories, from baby books to the most hard-edged, realistic teen fiction, are all about making sense of, and expressing wonder at, a big, sometimes frightening world. If you want to read fiction for children then you need to look at the world as if you were a child as well as a writer. Having access to your childhood self is useful for all writers – Graham Greene described childhood as a writer's capital – but for a writer of young people's fiction it is absolutely essential.

Exercise 45

Try taking your notebook to a public place – a library is a safe bet but you could try it in a shopping mall or a sports centre – and make yourself physically small. Sit on the floor and make detailed notes about how it feels to be looking up at everything and everyone.

Giving power to the weak

It's possible to say that there is an element of empowering the underdog in all great children's literature. It is unsurprising that children respond particularly well to stories where the weak emerge victorious. However loved and cared for, a child is always living under a dictatorship. The range of decisions they can make is limited. Their power is small compared with that of the adults around them. Literature for children should be subversive – a kind of protest song. In books children should make important life-changing decisions; they should have special powers whether these are supernatural or merely those that result from a keen wit. In other words, children should be at the centre of the world you create. Your universe should be a child's universe.

Of course some of you will be planning worlds where animals are at the centre, or toys or creatures entirely of your own devising. And this is fine. Not only fine, it's great, but I still say that it's the smaller animals, the tiniest creatures that should come out on top in the end.

Insight

Your heroes must always, always win. And your villains (probably adults) should suffer in inventive ways. Take Roald Dahl as a guide. Part of Dahl's appeal was not only that he

(Contd)

knew that people – including children – could be spiteful, cruel and idiotic, but that he was prepared to exaggerate these traits for the entertainment of his audience. And spite, cruelty and idiocy always prove the undoing of his villains.

Exercise 46

You'll love this. Make a list of all the people who have ever done you wrong. Now, next to their name, try and think of something that should happen to them. Make it comical if you can. Make it gory, grim and gruesome if you like. Try and make the punishment fit the crime. Revenge is a perfectly acceptable motive in all drama and children are very keen on justice. Aim for at least ten and you'll have enough incidents for several children's stories.

Revel in naughtiness

THE JOY OF RUDENESS

Underpants are always funny. We know this. So are bottoms. Children are innocently tickled by the things that adults seem embarrassed by. Aliens that steal underpants, dinosaurs that eat them, people who wear them on their heads. Surreal uses of the everyday and the vulgar will score points with the smaller crowd. Don't be afraid to fart, belch and have stomachs rumble at serious volume.

YOUR GUTS FOR GARTERS

'I'll have your guts for garters' was a favourite phrase of my grandmother's. I didn't understand it, but it sounded deliciously frightening. Exactly the effect that you might want to create in your audience. Children absolutely love blood and gore. Adults don't, however (or those reading to young children don't anyway). And they are at least half your audience. As a responsible writer of children's fiction you should make sure that any violence in your books is there for a reason, that it helps the story along. Yes, of course we want to frighten our audience a bit. Yes, we want to make them shiver. But we want them to enjoy the thrill of the rollercoaster we're giving them. We don't want them to feel sick and to want to get off. Whether you are Virginia Woolf or Dr Seuss, all writing is about getting readers to turn the page, hungry to find out what happens next. You don't want to terrify young readers.

Exercise 47

Think back to the most frightening moment you had as a child. Write it down as plainly and as simply as you can. Now write it down in a way that makes light of the situation somehow. Try writing it as a cartoon, or in rhyme. Or introduce something mad like a purple elephant floating into the story in a hot air balloon. The aim here is to surprise yourself as much as any younger readers.

EXTREME CHARACTERS

Extreme characters are fun to write and children's fiction would seem to be a natural home for them. Especially extremely nasty characters. Again, Roald Dahl is a good example of a writer who isn't constrained by the need to find redeeming features in his characters. In adult fiction people find it difficult to believe in someone who is wholly bad and even harder to enthuse about someone who is wholly good. Our heroes these days must be tainted by flaws which they endeavour to resolve by the end of the book, while our villains often have a reason for their moral turpitude. This isn't necessarily so with characters in children's books and this can be hugely liberating.

I said right at the beginning of this book that writing was play, that it should be fun, that essentially it was 'What if…' and 'Let's pretend…', and producing larger than life characters is part of the joy of fiction for kids. Everything can be bigger, brighter, more black and white than would be acceptable in the greyer, more psychologically accurate world of writing for adults.

The problem of problems

Part of the point of reading is to make sense of the world you're in. To try out different ways of being. This is especially important for children who are travelling without maps a lot of the time. When a problem comes up in our lives there is a good chance that we have a storehouse of solutions to draw on. And if not, then there will be places and people we can go to who have the requisite experience. Children often have the choice of blind faith in peers, family or teachers, or trying to work things out on their own. It's a difficult world and being a child is not for the timid. There are real and emotional dangers at every turn. And books, like the best films and the best television, or like a conversation with a good friend, can present children with dilemmas and choices in a safe way. Identifying with the struggles of a character in a book (even if that character is a lonely pig or a homesick dinosaur!) can also be a valuable way for a child to develop empathy and emotional literacy.

DON'T PREACH

But children also hate being lectured. They get enough of being told what to do, so they are going to be naturally resistant to being told what to think. Stories where it is obvious that there is a didactic intent are likely to be little loved by children, however laudable their aims. It is hard for an author to create a character that engages if that character owes their place on the page to the need to teach the readers a lesson. Children sometimes love their teachers, but they rarely love a teacher's pet. And the characters that are in the book to show us exactly how we should or shouldn't behave are going to be the worst kinds of characters. They are going to be wooden and lifeless. And we won't trust them.

I began my working life teaching drama to troubled children and it seemed that every week we were being encouraged to set up anti-bullying workshops where children would be asked to devise stories around bullying that ended happily. All the children I ever taught could dream up any number of scenarios where a bully was eventually defeated by the actions of defiant kids acting in concert with their noble teachers, but it didn't seem to make much difference to the actual incidence of bullying. The workshops had simply become another lesson with a 'right answer' that had to be given in order to keep 'Sir' happy. Good children's books are driven by conflict and problem solving but they need surprise, and too many issue-based books lack this essential element.

A good way to make sure that the problems your characters overcome are real is to make sure that the problems arise naturally from their characters. In other words, create the characters in detail so that you know them intimately (this is just as important if your characters are rabbits or moles or rats or any other creature real or imagined, or mythological for that matter!), and the themes, issues and how they deal with them will then come out in an organic, unforced way.

Exercise 48

Try to think of a moral or a message that you consider important for children to learn. Now come up with a short storyline (keep it to just one page of A4) that illustrates this, involving two or more characters. Now write detailed character descriptions of those characters. Write down absolutely everything you can think of. Make sure you get in all their likes and dislikes. Now revisit your storyline and inhabit it with the fully rounded characters. Remember the rule: you need to know everything about your character's history. When it comes to the story, however, the readers don't.

Illustrations

Unless you are a very talented artist don't bother doing the drawings for any of your stories yourself. Nor should you get a friend to illustrate them (unless your friend is genuinely gifted in this area). If your story comes to the notice of a publisher they will probably want to choose an illustrator themselves, someone who fits with their house style and who they are used to working with. They've already taken a big chance by accepting your work; it's asking a lot to get them to take on a new illustrator too.

Poetry for children

Children love rhythm and rhyme. They also love alliteration, onomatopoeia, puns and wordplay of all kinds. Part of the joy of writing for children is that exuberant verse finds ready appreciation. Clever or outrageous rhymes and vivid imagery as well as a gripping narrative can greatly endear a book to a child. You don't want to make it too obvious however. You want to pile surprise on surprise for your audience. In general a good rule is to go for the third rhyme that you think of. The first is one that children might think of for themselves. The second is one that their parents will think of. The third rhyme that occurs to you may be the original, startling one that delights. It may also be the word that prompts you to take your story in directions that surprise even you, the writer.

Sharing stories

Insight

You are the most important element in the story. You don't need to be young to be a great writer of children's stories. You do need to be able to stay connected to the child inside yourself.

You need to identify with that girl who got left out of games at playtime, or the boy who fell off his bike. But it is *your* ideas and, most importantly, *your* passions and enthusiasms that will come off the page and engage younger readers.

Remember, children aren't the same as us. They are not cynical or distrustful. They expect to be liked and admired. They expect that people will find their stories fascinating and in return they expect that you are a nice, friendly entertaining person with a fund of stories of your own. And they are right. Spend time with children and you will want to make yourself worthy of their trust in you. And you will want your stories to be treasured too and you will work hard to make them as good as they can be because this audience really does deserve the best of you.

Exercise 49

Here's the final test in this section. Write a story for your chosen age group. Spend a lot of time on it, just as you would on a story for adults. Read it aloud to yourself. Put it away for a while, then redraft it. Then put it away again and redraft it again. Get a candid constructive reader friend to make suggestions. Redraft it again. Now get a child of the right age group to read it. Make any more necessary changes. Now comes the crucial test: read it to a small group of the right age group at a nearby school or youth group (it should be obvious that you have to get all the proper authorities to agree through all the right channels). Elicit their honest reactions and solicit suggestions for how it could be improved. As with any advice you are free to ignore it. Some of it will no doubt be contradictory anyway, but what you can't ignore is the feeling in the room. That never lies. You will be able to tell if your story is holding the attention of its target audience. However well behaved your audience are, if their concentration is faltering then

(Contd)

a dozen tiny rustlings and fidgetings and whisperings will let you know. Even if the kids are silent there will be something about the dead quality of the air that will tell you which parts have failed to grab them. Similarly, the atmosphere will become subtly charged if your story is doing its job.

Some of you will be better readers and performers than others. But it is part of a writer's job to be able to read their own work well, I think. If you are not a natural performer it really is worth putting the hours in and improving. It is something you can learn with practice and repetition.

Professional tip from Lee Weatherly

To write for children you need to cast yourself back to your childhood self. It's not enough to observe children and then try to write about them from the outside in; you need to feel it yourself, from the inside out. Rediscover play; walk silently through the woods and wonder; ask 'what if?'. Being a children's writer doesn't really have anything to do with having *children; it's all about connecting with those feelings within yourself – and then writing them.*

Lee Weatherly is the author of *Child X* (David Fickling Books).

10 THINGS TO REMEMBER

1 *Children deserve the best.*

2 *A good children's book will also engage adults.*

3 *Spend as much time with children as you can.*

4 *Write stories that give power to the weak.*

5 *Revel in rudeness.*

6 *Don't preach.*

7 *Create some extreme characters.*

8 *Children love rhythm, rhyme and alliteration.*

9 *Learn how to read and perform your work.*

10 *Read as much modern children's fiction as you can.*

10

....

Starting to write a novel

In this chapter you will learn:
- *about the exciting challenge the novel offers you*
- *how to kick-start your book*
- *how to decide on a central character*
- *the importance of voice*
- *the basics of structure.*

> *A novel is nothing less than the subtlest instrument for self-examination and self-display that mankind has invented yet.*
>
> John Updike

The challenge

Because writing a novel is such a big challenge, and because so many writers want to achieve it, you'll find a large chunk of this book is concerned with novel-writing. You may not have begun working your way through this programme with the idea that you would become a novelist, but my experience is that the novel is the ultimate dream of most writers.

Of all the courses I have organized over the years, those that deal with novel-writing are the most in demand. If, after tackling the exercises in the following chapters you don't want to write novels, then I still believe that you have completed an important part of a writer's journey. That is, deciding what kind of writer you are.

In any case, I'm not sure that I believe you. As far as I can tell all playwrights, screenwriters, journalists and children's writers and bloggers, still want to pit themselves against the challenge of writing a novel. Only some poets – and perhaps some short story writers – seem immune to this siren call.

THE EXPLORATION BEGINS

Insight

Every new novel is a vast and undiscovered continent. And every journey through that continent is a partnership between your conscious and the deeper, hidden parts of your psyche.

Your subconscious and your rational mind will move forward through this new territory together, often arguing about the roads to take. Your subconscious will want to drive to the darkest places, while your rational brain will want to take easier routes, cut down obstacles, build roads and generally impose order on chaos. Your unconscious is a pioneer and your conscious self is like a colonial administrator, attempting to impose carefully constructed systems on this difficult, lawless territory.

And there's the question of population too. Of all the real-life continents a novel might resemble, the best example is probably Australia. When your novel begins to take shape it is a land which you, as an explorer, know nothing about. The first thing you notice is that it seems a wild place, but abundant too, rich in possibilities. And then you'll start transporting a population into it. But on the journey to the new world these characters have been growing too. It seems they've got plans independent of whatever you've got in mind for them and within moments of landing some or all of your characters have escaped into the wilderness. Others, for whom you had high hopes, won't survive.

As you and your people travel further into the continent you'll find the landscape is also different from what you thought. It's full of mirages, false trails. You'll find too that this landscape is already peopled by an indigenous population who must be taken account of. They have their own demands and their own way of being which perhaps fits this place better than the characters you are trying to import.

And when, after months of struggle, the novel has been created, when the dust of all the arguments between your conscious and your subconscious has settled and there is a definite land mapped out and on the page, that land will seem altogether more vast and more complex than you thought possible. And yet... and yet... the fact that it is not the place you thought it was, will nag at you. You'll want to tinker and fix, and in fixing find that you've upset the whole ecosystem of this new world. Then, when trying to fix these imbalances you will find others that need fixing too and so on, until eventually you must leave it alone because there are other worlds to explore, other novels that need your attention.

It's at this point that readers begin to tramp through and they will see a different place from you. They will bring their own histories, their own prejudices, and their own characters. Some, like inquisitive backpackers, will want to get away from the roads through the novel you have created for them; they will be more interested in places that you yourself hardly noticed were there. Others will drift without comment past the beautiful parts of this world, the bits that you yourself are most proud of, seemingly in a hurry just to get to the end of the tour.

CHARACTER CREDENTIALS

> **Insight**
>
> What I am trying to show is that building a novel is perhaps the greatest challenge a writer can embark upon. You need all the skills of a diplomat with the drive, tenacity and ruthless efficiency of a megalomaniac.

In writing a novel you are literally playing God. And you've got to be the God of the Old Testament: ruthless, jealous, capricious and generous. But, unlike the Old Testament God, there comes a time when you are no longer the judge, but are instead judged. When you are not Almighty, but are instead in the hands of the readers and you'll find them far more capricious than any mere deity. At least, it will feel that way.

It is also, of course, hugely rewarding and hugely exciting. As you embark on the journey of the novel you are Shackleton, Captain Scott, Edmund Hillary, David Livingstone, Columbus, Neil Armstrong, Captain Cook, Ellen MacArthur and Nelson Mandela. You are a statesman–explorer and you don't even have to leave your living room.

First steps

A straight literary novel is between 70,000 and 200,000 words, with most coming in at about 100,000. And before starting down this long road you need to decide what kind of book you are going to write. I don't simply mean what genre are you going to write in – are you writing crime, historical, romantic, science or literary fiction – but what is your book going to be about? And why does it need to be written?

Exercise 50

In not more than 100 words, write down exactly why you want to write a novel and who you hope will read it. This will help clarify in your mind your aims and objectives.

Insight

There are about a million manuscripts in the offices of London or New York literary agents at any one time. Only a fraction of these get published. Don't let that put you off, however. None of those novels is your novel. None of them

(Contd)

are written with your voice. None of them say what only you can say. But it is best to be clear about what exactly it is you want to say and why the novel is the best way to say it.

The theme

What is your story going to be about? This is a single word or a short phrase that encapsulates the essence of the story. Being clear about this right at the outset, before you've thought about plot, setting or characters, will help you stay focused and prevent your novel becoming a sprawling mess. It will prevent you being led off at tangents and into cul-de-sacs. It will, with any luck, save you time later when it comes to editing (it probably won't but you can always hope). Dianne Doubtfire put it well when she said that 'A book without a theme can become a mere sequence of events with no foundation, no reason for existence.'

Insight
Whatever your theme is, keep it in your mind's eye as a light to guide you through the path of your story.

Your theme will probably be something that you have personal experience of. A passionate desire to communicate experience and knowledge will give your book an inner heat, a propulsive motor that will keep it going.

But a novel is not an autobiography and having your theme shining ahead of you as you write will help you cut out those parts of your life story that don't fit. It will also help as a reminder to make sure that you alter details of your life as you need to. Like a good tabloid editor, you mustn't let the facts get in the way of a good story. As I've said before, 'Write what you know' is good advice for a writer but so is its opposite: 'Write what you don't know' – this can be important too. Making stuff up is part of a fiction writer's job and one you shouldn't shy away from. One important difference between fictive lives and our own lives is that in fiction everything has to mean something. This is often not the case in real life.

Exercise 51

Write down five themes that you feel qualified to tackle. Now circle two of these as contenders for the theme of your first book.

Viewpoints

I touched on the problem of deciding whether to write in the first or third person back when discussing short stories in Chapter 4, and the problem is magnified in the novel. For one thing, you have so many more choices. You can, for example, do both in different parts of the novel. You can have multiple narrators telling different stories within the novel, or telling the same story from differing perspectives. Or you can, as Bill Broady did in his very successful novella *Swimmer*, use the second person and address your story to a mysterious 'you'. The choices are yours, but I would offer some advice.

Conventional wisdom has it that the easiest kind of book to write is one with an omniscient third-person narrator. A God figure able to see into the minds of all the characters and able to follow them all. I disagree. I like a limited narrator who only has access to parts of the story. As a new novelist I would be inclined to keep things simple. Match ambition to your limited experience. Admittedly, this will give you some problems later on because you can only tell the reader things that your narrator would know. You can only get to know the characters through him or her. But this very straitjacket means that you are forced to keep things tightly focused.

Insight

If you have *more* than one narrator, what you will find is that readers prefer some voices to others.

Readers' attention will flag a little when a narrator takes over who they don't warm to. This happens even in great books like Jonathan Franzen's *The Corrections* or Irvine Welsh's *Trainspotting*, both of which are first-person novels told by more than one character. In Franzen's book the story takes place over many years and is told by various members of a dysfunctional family, while Welsh's novel is narrated by the various denizens of an Edinburgh housing estate. Great novels, great voices, but still some narrators appeal more than others.

My own first novel, *Tag*, is narrated in turn by a 40-year-old male high school teacher and a 15-year-old girl who is a working-class tearaway. People seemed to like both voices but nearly everyone preferred the voice of Colleen, my feisty hooligan. Bafflingly, they also thought Colleen's voice rang the most true. Obviously my inner teenage girl had been desperate to be let out for years and so she seized the chance when she got it. Jonathan Diamond, my other narrator, was maybe slightly slower off the mark. Again, this is another reminder of how important it can be not to be too hamstrung by sticking solely to what you know when beginning your book. Observation and empathy will take you a long way.

Whose story is it?

There is a saying that 'character is story'. It is the characters that will drive your plot. But not all characters will have equal weight. Your novel is not a democracy. Even if you decide to write in the third person you will still need to have a central character in whom the readers can invest their emotional energy. Even if this central character is unlikeable, evil even, we want to see the world through their eyes.

Insight

Just as it is easier with a first book to stick to the first person and a theme that you have experience of, it is probably also a help to have a likeable – if flawed – central character. Too nice and we won't find them plausible or interesting, but if they are too unlikeable then we will become irritated. We won't want to spend much time in their company.

We will turn to characterization in Chapter 12, but it is probably worth having at least an outline of your dramatis personae even at this early stage.

Exercise 52

Keeping your theme in mind, write brief character sketches for six of your principal characters (any more than six major characters and you risk losing control of them entirely). Now who, out of this collection, deserves to be the central character? Who is going to be the hero of this book? Choose carefully because this person is going to stay with you night and day for months or years. They are going to have to be fascinating to you now, and grow more fascinating as the story develops. Having the wrong central character is probably what prevents first novels getting off the ground more than almost any other fault (except, possibly, over-ambition).

THE VOICE

Finding the voice of your central character is key to unlocking the story. A strong, engaging voice propels the storyline and hooks the reader in: Rob, the melancholy music obsessive in Nick Hornby's *High Fidelity*; Judith Bastiaanz, the naïve young Dutch émigré to the New World whose disastrous first infatuation helps destroy her family in Kathryn Heyman's *The Accomplice*; the dizzy but determined Bridget in Helen Fielding's *Bridget Jones's Diary*; Holden Caulfield in J. D. Salinger's *Catcher in the Rye*, the prototype of every moody teenage narrator we have had since the 1950s (Caulfield's direct descendant is the unlucky Vernon in D. B. C. Pierre's Booker Prize-winning *Vernon God Little*); Bessy Buckley, the wide-eyed, sassy nineteenth-century hero in Jane Harris's *The Observations* has a rollicking voice that carries the whole novel; Christopher, the maths prodigy with Asperger's Syndrome in Mark Haddon's groundbreaking *The Curious Incident of the Dog in the Night-time*; the earnest and wise Scout in *To Kill A Mockingbird*. All of these strike me as good examples of stories where a strong narrative voice has been established right at the beginning of the book and sustained through to the end. There are countless others, however. All of the characters mentioned above have flaws (except just possibly the child, Scout) but none of them are unlikeable. Holden Caulfield can seem alienated and difficult but that is exactly why he exercises such a pull on the psyche of generations of teenagers.

The point is that these narrators have a voice which is vivid, alive and unique. They all share the fact that they look at the world in unusual, albeit very different ways.

Voice is probably the hardest of skills to master. It is certainly the hardest to explain, which is why I've reached for so many different examples. It's important to get it right. A wrong note in the voice of your narrator and you will quickly begin to lose the trust of your readership.

Insight

The Californian writer Peter Plate has this to say about voice/style: 'Look for repetitions, rhythm, cadence, pacing (setting something up, bringing it to a close). Look for texture in sentences.'

Even if you have made the decision to write your book in the third person, you will still need to have a voice. An invisible narrator is actually impossible: readers will be responding to a narrative voice whether or not it is that of an actual character. Voice in this context may be a synonym for style. Look at the novels of Fay Weldon or E. L. Doctorow to see how the third-person novel still requires the push of a powerful narrative voice.

Exercise 53

Experiment with the voices of your central characters. Have each of them recount an incident from their childhood in their own words. This will be a good way to test whether or not your central character is the right one. Try and make their voices as distinct from each other as you can.

Insight

Don't write in dialect. Accents and dialect should be implied by the choice of vocabulary. Unless you're Irvine Welsh, writing out accents phonetically doesn't really work. Even if you *are* Irvine Welsh it doesn't always work (his London characters are never as convincing in terms of their accent as his Scottish ones).

Structure

Aspiring writers worry about structure more than they worry about anything else. It's as though the word 'structure' holds the same sense of arcane unknowable magic as the words 'quantum physics'. And yet the mechanics of story structure are relatively straightforward. Most books, plays, films and television dramas are written with a three act structure. And this phrase in itself seems to be a posh way of saying: Beginning, Middle and End.

THREE ACTS, THREE KINDS OF PLOT

The plot is the journey of your characters through these three acts. There are, essentially, three kinds of plot. The first is the most familiar.

The linear plot
A linear plot is where the action moves straightforwardly through the acts, the tension building until a climax in the final act. This kind of plotting is familiar to us from many an action movie, as well as many classic novels.

The other two kinds of plot are cyclic. In other words the position at the end of the book resembles that at the start, except that all the characters are utterly changed.

The heroic cycle
Familiar to us from the great epics such as *King Arthur* or *The Odyssey*, this follows the pattern of: Departure, Initiation and Return (think of the structure of *The Hobbit*).

The mythic journey
This can be expressed as: Cage, Escape, Quest, Dragon and Home (think of the structure of *Watership Down* – warned by a vision of impending catastrophe a group of young rabbits decide to leave their threatened warren (Cage); they get away despite the best and brutal efforts of the authorities to stop them (Escape); they then search for exactly the right place to set up a new warren (Quest), defeating the fearsome Nazi warren run by General Woundwort (Dragon); finally they end their days in bounty, together with the does they liberated from the enemy warren (Home).

Another way of thinking about this kind of structure might be as three acts containing five parts, these parts being: Inciting incident, Complication, Betrayal, Climax and Resolution. Act One would contain the Inciting incident and the Complication, things heat up with a Betrayal in Act Two, and Act Three would contain the Climax but also the Resolution.

We'll say more about plotting in Chapter 13, but you might like to try this exercise now.

Exercise 54

Take your central character on a journey using one or more of the plot types described above. What type is going to best suit your theme? Just sketch it out for now.

Setting

This is where your novel takes place and when. Again, I have devoted the whole of Chapter 11 to these key considerations but it is worth thinking a little about this right at the planning stage of your novel.

Exercise 55

You have a theme and a collection of characters and a rough idea of the type of journey that they might undertake. You might want to jot down now the kind of locations where scenes might take place.

Insight

Novels are best written in scenes. We don't need to know everything that happens in your character's life. We want the important moments, and the setting for these important moments is going to be crucial.

GET YOUR FACTS STRAIGHT

You will want to choose the kinds of settings that you yourself know well. If you know Edinburgh and you know council offices then utilize this knowledge. Likewise if you know college radio stations and you know Berkeley then utilize that knowledge too. The reader will want to trust that you know what you're talking about. The same is true of historical periods: if you are writing a novel about the past then you owe it to your readers to have researched thoroughly the time in which your book is set. This is true even if you lived through the era about which you are writing. The memory is an unreliable muscle and you will need to go and check your facts. Make sure that you have the right prime minister in power, or that people really were sending emails in 1993.

You will also want to avoid clichés about historical periods. For example a cliché about the 1980s is that it was all Gordon Gecko and Greed is Good, with the whole nation in thrall to earning money at the expense of everybody else. And yet what I remember from the 1980s is the dole, the *Socialist Worker* sellers at tube stations, the first appearance of beggars on British streets in hundreds of years, and strikes. Nobody I knew was wearing braces and making a killing on the stock market.

In a similar way the 1960s is often portrayed as the decade of free love and explosive social change. And for an elite that might have been true. But for most people the sexual liberation didn't happen until later as the changes in social mores only gradually filtered out from London and the West Coast of the USA.

TIME PERIODS

Another big decision to make is over what time period your story is going to unfold. Is it over decades, as with the classic great American novels like *The World According To Garp*? Or is it just one day, like James Joyce's *Ulysses* or Ian McEwan's *Saturday*?

Whatever you decide, thinking about how the weather changes and how the seasons affect the lives of your characters will help give you a sense of how your story might unfold. Farmers are perhaps the most affected by these kinds of changes, but shopkeepers must plan for Christmas and Halloween. School teachers plan for examination periods. Everyone is affected by the nights drawing in and the weather getting colder and wetter. In India, or America, or Africa, the seasons are different and will affect your characters in different ways. The rhythm of the world they inhabit must impact on your characters in some way.

Teach something

For many, part of the pleasure of reading novels is learning. In a great novel one will learn about the world, about human nature, about oneself and about different time periods. But there are other more low-key pleasures to be had. The novels of John Murray teach about contemporary Cumbria, a place to which, shamefully, I have never been; *The Electric Michelangelo* by Sarah Hall is fascinating on the evolution of tattooing; the novels of George Macdonald Fraser are the best kind of historical writing, with painstakingly researched facts set in the context of exhilarating action; *Trainspotting* is fascinating on the world of Scottish junkies; while Nicholas Royle's *Antwerp* brings to vivid life the demi-monde of a city which no one outside of Belgium knows very much about.

If you have special knowledge about something, whether it is breeding pedigree cats or manufacturing class A drugs, then I suggest that giving the readers access to this kind of information is actually a kind of generosity.

Story, story, story

It often comes as something of a shock to those who attend writing courses that 80,000 beautiful words do not make a novel.

I have said that your characters generate the story and this is true. But you are not writing lengthy character studies. There must be constant movement, ceaseless surprising progressions. Just as much modern music now seeks to wring the maximum out of each chord before moving a tune forward, thus sacrificing melody and urgency, so many emerging novelists forget that what keeps us turning pages is a story.

Novelists, even the most serious ones, are in the entertainment business. We are purveyors of pleasure as well as knowledge. It is a complicated, complex kind of pleasure but pleasure nevertheless. Ford Madox Ford wrote that each line of the novel should push it forward. Things have to happen, your characters need to make things happen and then respond to things that other characters do and say. They can't stand still and they shouldn't reflect for too long or too often, unless reflecting for too long is part of their essence in which case it should have troubling consequences for them. A novel is a sophisticated form of fairground. In the hands of a good novelist you should get the visceral thrills of the rollercoaster, combined with the darker arts of the illusionist. Things have to happen.

> **Insight**
> Go back to those books you love for their quieter, more reflective qualities and note down what actually happens in each book. You'll be surprised how many deaths, infidelities and hurts of all kinds there are. Even in Anne Tyler, even in Jane Austen come to that.

Don't get it right, get it written

I don't know who said this first. I'd like to think it was me but it almost certainly wasn't. It is excellent advice for those starting out on the journey of the novel, however. Too many new writers begin their first chapter in the white heat of creativity and then polish and hone and tweak that opening over and over until it's shining.

In the meantime months have passed and the momentum of the story has been lost.

Bash it down; get it on the page. Forget the critic on your shoulder who has tried to stop you doing anything worthwhile since you were born, and is not helpful at this stage in your life. You will go back and edit and change and tweak and redraft and suffer all the agonies associated with that stage, but for now you need to draw up a realistic schedule for blasting out that first draft. Let it burst out without worrying about coherence or structure or spelling or paragraphing. Get it done. Get it out of you. The real work of the novelist begins with the redrafting. As the poet David Harsent says, 'All writing is rewriting.' Nevertheless, a bit of planning will help you put your first draft down with minimal risk of becoming blocked.

Exercise 56

You're serious about writing a novel so draw up a plan of campaign. Set yourself a deadline. Think about how long you've got to write this novel. (Don't put 'the rest of my life'. I regularly meet people on the courses we run who tell me they have spent nearly ten years on a book. That kind of confession makes my blood run cold.) You'll need time to plot, time to develop your characters, time to work on the setting, time to write a synopsis and then you'll need to write a first draft. And of course you'll need time to do all the other things in your life – work, family, exercise. Writing your novel shouldn't cost you any of these, that's too high a price to pay.

Of course you should have a writing routine established by now. Break the task of getting this novel down into chunks and stick to the schedule you've set yourself, whether that is six weeks of planning, followed by a chapter a week, or another schedule which is manageable for you. Write it on the calendar and pin it somewhere prominent.

Insight

Tell as many people as possible that you are writing a novel. This makes all those who might sabotage your plans part of the team. If people feel involved in your struggle they might not be so insistent about breaking into your writing time.

The following chapters take the major elements of fiction writing and provide detailed exercises on each of them. You can work on them alongside the novel you are planning, or come back to the novel after having completed them. Or go to them whenever you get stuck on a particular aspect of your book. This chapter has been about starts and springboards. If all has gone to plan then you should be ready to begin a first chapter.

Exercise 57

Write the first chapter of your novel. Don't give everything away at once. Remember what Charles Reade wrote in his nineteenth-century writing manual *Advice to young authors on writing novels*, 'Make 'em laugh; make 'em cry; make 'em wait.'

Professional tip from Jeremy Sheldon

While you're still developing your craft, don't be tempted to deal with too many main characters. Many good storylines are founded on a network of relationships between two or three central characters and prove that there's certainly enough in such a situation for intelligent and insightful writing. Focusing on a small cast of characters makes it easier to control and explore the dramatic conflicts in the story, and to control things like point of view.

Jeremy Sheldon is the author of *The Comfort Zone* and *The Smiling Affair* (both Cape).

10 THINGS TO REMEMBER

1 *A novel is usually around 100,000 words.*

2 *100,000 beautiful words do not a novel make – there must be a story as well.*

3 *Don't write in dialect.*

4 *Have a theme (even if you are the only one who knows it).*

5 *Write your novel in scenes.*

6 *Teach the reader something.*

7 *Use either the heroic cycle or the mythic journey as a basis for your plot and know the difference.*

8 *Don't get it right, get it written.*

9 *Try to have a likeable hero.*

10 *Make 'em laugh, make 'em cry, make 'em wait.*

Setting

In this chapter you will learn:
- *the role setting should play in your story*
- *how to decide between real and imaginary settings*
- *how to develop a visual style.*

Without a sense of place the work is often reduced to a cry of voices in empty rooms, a literature of the self, at its best poetic music; at its worst a thin gruel of the ego.

William Kennedy

The importance of place

The places in which your stories take place can be vital to their success. In many of the best novels the setting is almost a character in the book. The India of Forster's *A Passage To India*, the Edinburgh of Ian Rankin's detective novels, the Yorkshire moorland of *Wuthering Heights*, the small towns and suburbs of the USA brought to life by John Updike, the island in William Golding's *Lord of the Flies*: all of these are stories where the texture of the setting illuminates the action and the characters.

CITYSCAPES

Some settings have been used over and over again by different writers because they exercise an irresistible pull on the imagination.

Venice for example is one huge, floating metaphor with its combination of the highest human art and the murky waters on which it is perched. On the one hand there is St Mark's Square, with its awe-inspiring church, and piazzas and palaces, but everywhere too there is the rough and tumble of ordinary life. And there's the fact that the city itself, raised in defiance of nature, is beginning to crack and crumble, threatening always to throw the fine buildings with all their ornamentation and excess under the waves. Yet somehow, it continues to survive. No wonder it was the favourite setting for Shakespeare and his friends. Whenever they wanted a backdrop against which to set a story of vice, greed, sensuality and deceit, Venice was always the first place they went to.

There are other cities and places which seem destined to inspire writers. London, Paris, New York: all that teeming humanity from all corners of the world squashed together in a few square miles, it's bound to be a rich seam of stories. Anywhere where different cultures clash is going to be exciting to a novelist. Berlin was a favourite setting before the war and then again during the Cold War when it was on the frontline between capitalist West and Soviet-dominated East. It captured the imagination of scores of thriller writers. Places on the border between different worlds are also intriguing locations.

THE EVERYDAY

It isn't simply landscapes that can provide evocative locations: the hospital ward in Ken Kesey's *One Flew Over the Cuckoo's Nest*; the oppressive school in Zoë Heller's *Notes on a Scandal*. Both of these institutional settings help brew a feeling of claustrophobia in which the characters are trapped. The settings are so authentically drawn that we feel we can trust the writer to pilot us skilfully through the plot too.

Don't worry if you think that your chosen settings are too bleak or too unromantic. The grim English steel town of Corby was the setting for John Burnside's aptly titled *Living Nowhere*, a novel that works precisely because of the sense of small-town, dead-end ennui that rises from the pages.

IMAGINARY LOCATIONS

As we've said before, it helps if your setting is a place that you know well, but some places you are inventing from scratch and with these it is, paradoxically, all the more important that you get them right. If you get a street name wrong in a real town people will no doubt write you a pained letter, but if your world is entirely fictitious then it must feel truthful.

In creating a new world you don't have the luxury of looking places up on an A–Z street map. You must overcome the reader's natural scepticism about things that are obviously made-up by giving them a fully realized place. It must feel that you at least have been there, even if no one else has. And of course, like the set in a film, it mustn't be so distracting as to take our minds away from the story.

Interweaving a sense of place so that it adds to the momentum of a novel is one of the most difficult tricks for a novelist to pull off.

Examples of a visual style

Here are three examples of writers who combine character and setting extremely well.

For forty-two years, Lewis and Benjamin Jones slept side by side, in their parents' bed, at their farm which was known as 'The Vision'.

The bedstead, an oak four poster, came from their mother's home at Brynn-Draenog when she married in 1899. Its faded cretonne hangings, printed with a design of larkspur and roses, shut out the mosquitoes of summer, and the draughts in winter.

Callused heels had worn holes in the linen sheets, and parts of the patchwork quilt had frayed. Under the goose-feather mattress, there was a second mattress of horsehair, and this had sunk into two troughs, leaving a ridge between the sleepers.

The room was always dark and smelled of lavender and mothballs.

The smell of mothballs came from a pyramid of hatboxes piled up beside the washstand. On the bed-table lay a pin-cushion still stuck with Mrs Jones' hatpins, and on the end wall hung an engraving of Holman Hunt's 'Light of the World', in an ebonized frame.

One of the windows looked out over the green fields of England: the other looked back into Wales, past a clump of larches, at the Black Hill.

On the Black Hill by Bruce Chatwin (Vintage Classics)

And here's another opening – very different in style and in the first person this time – from A. L. Kennedy.

How it happens is a long story, always.

And I apparently begin with being here: a boxy room that's too wide to be cosy, its dirty ceiling hung just low enough to press down an unmistakeable haze of claustrophobia. To my right is an over-large clock of the kind favoured by playschools and homes for the elderly, the kind with bold, black numbers and cartoon-thick hands that effectively shout what time it is whether you're curious or not. It shows 8.42 and counting. Above is a generalized sting of yellow light.

8.42.

But I don't know which one – night or morning. Either way, from what I can already see, I would rather not be involved in this too far beyond 8.43.

In one fist, I notice, I'm holding a key. Its fob is made of
viciously green plastic, translucent and moulded to a shape
which illustrates what would happen if a long-dead ear were
inflated until morbidly obese. I only know that it's actually
meant to be a leaf, because it is marked with an effort
towards the stem, the ribs and veins that a leaf might have.
I presume that I'm meant to like this key and give it the
benefit of the doubt because people are fond of trees and,
by extension, leaves. But I don't like leaves, not even
real ones.

Paradise by A. L. Kennedy (Vintage)

The final example in this section, again in the third person, is by
Sarah Hall from her Booker prize shortlisted novel *The Electric*
Michelangelo and describes an English seaside resort in surprising
and compelling terms.

He looked up and out to the horizon. The large, smeary
bay window revealed a desolate summer scene. The tide
was a long way out, further than he could see, as far as
anyone knew it was gone for good and had left the town
permanently inland. It took a lot of trust to believe the
water would ever come back each day, all that distance,
it seemed like an awful amount of labour for no good
reason. The whole dirty, grey-shingled beach was now
bare, except for one or two souls out for a stroll, and one
or two hardy sunbathers, in their two-shilling-hire deck
chairs, determined to make the most of their annual holiday
week away from the mills, the mines and the foundries
of the north. A week to take in the bracing salty air and
perhaps, if they were blessed, the sun would make a cheerful
appearance and rid them of their pallor. A week to remove
all the coal and metal dust and chaff and smoke from their
lungs and to be a consolation for their perpetual ill-health,
the chest diseases they would eventually inherit and often
die from, the shoddy eyesight, swollen arthritic fingers,
allergies, calluses, deafness, all the squalid cousins of their
trade. One way to tell where you were in this town, should

you ever forget where you were, should you ever go mad and
begin not to recognize the obvious scenery, the hotels, the
choppy water, the cheap tea rooms, pie and pea restaurants,
fish and chip kiosks, the amusement arcades, and the
dancehalls on the piers, one way to verify your location was
to watch the way the visitors breathed. There was method to
it. Deliberation. They put effort into it. Their chests rose and
fell like furnace bellows. So as to make the most of whatever
they could snort down into them.

The Electric Michelangelo by Sarah Hall (Faber and Faber)

All three of these very different pieces build their overall impression
and effect by focusing on a collage of details, small in themselves,
that cumulatively build up a powerful sense of place. At the same
time all three guide us towards a sense of the characters, and the
kind of story that might begin to emerge. The setting is not static.
The description of the place is alive, populated and already moving
the narrative along.

Exercise 58

Try and continue one of the stories above in a similar style.
Aim for a further 100 words or so.

Exercise 59

1   *Go to one of your favourite places and try to take a*
    good, long, close look at all the details that make it
    special. Imagine that you are seeing it for the first time.
    What you are trying to do is collect a list of all the details
    that when put together will make a precise evocation of
    the place. Don't forget to include people in your notes.

(Contd)

2   *Now try and imagine why someone might dislike this place that you love so much. Would there be details that would infuriate them, or make them sad?*

Exercise 60

Next, think about someone you know well. It can even be a character from a story you are writing. Imagine that they are in your house. What would they see? What would be the details that they pick up on? Now take that character into your childhood home. What would they see now? What impression would that house make?

The next exercise was given to me by Martyn Bedford, the author of *Black Cat*, *The Houdini Girl* and *Island of Lost Souls* among others. Martyn has also taught creative writing for many years and is an incredibly talented and generous tutor.

Exercise 61

Your character is making a journey home after a long time away. They can be travelling by bus, train, car, taxi, plane, on foot, by boat, bike... it's up to you. Write a scene, in the third person, in which you interweave the exploration of their thoughts with the description of the unfolding images of the journey as the character nears their destination. Bear in mind, this is not merely an exercise in the evocation of place, but in portraying the relationship between character and place. We should see the setting through the character's eyes, infused with their impressions and preoccupations.

Describing imaginary places can be one of the most satisfying aspects of the fiction writer's job. So much so that it is often one of the areas where we are apt to get carried away and ladle on far too much. The readers start to buckle under the strain of it and their heads start to throb with sensory overload. With descriptions of setting, like so much else in both life and writing, less is more. Limit yourself. Try and make a habit of interspersing description with action.

Here's one last example, from Iris Murdoch this time.

> *He pulled back the curtain a little and looked out into the November evening. Snow had begun to fall again in Ebury Street, large snow flakes moving densely, steadily, with visible silence, in the light of the street lamps, and crowding dimly above in the windless dark. A few cars hissed by, their sound muted and softened. The count was heard to say, 'It's snowing,' but checked himself. When someone is dying there is no point in telling him about the snow. There was no more weather for Guy.*
>
> Nuns and Soldiers by Iris Murdoch (Penguin Books Limited)

Describing snowfall is difficult for a writer: sentiment and cliché are too often a temptation. Here, however, Murdoch pulls it off splendidly while at the same time giving us an insight both into the character of the protagonist and the situation he finds himself in.

Insight
Don't ever be tempted to describe the dust motes floating in a beam of sunlight coming through a window in the morning. According to one of my friends, who is a top publisher, nearly all the novels submitted to her feature such an image. It's worn out and hackneyed and you must be ruthless in striking out any stale, overworked images.

Professional tip from Monique Roffey

Never underestimate the importance of place and its impact on the lives and emotions of your characters. All any novice writer needs to do is read the first chapter of The Grapes of Wrath *to know about the importance of place in fiction. In it, Steinbeck sets up place, the Oklahoma dust bowl, as a major source of unrelenting conflict. Place is the raison d'être of the characters; they fight to survive there. It is the reason for their journey away. The whole book is about their journey. Places have names, they have smells, sounds and climates. Place is the home of the novel. Never forget to fill the reader in on just where the characters are: Mars, Newfoundland, or the throbbing dance floor at Studio 51 in 1970s New York.*

Monique Roffey is the author of *The White Woman on the Green Bicycle* (Simon & Schuster).

5 THINGS TO REMEMBER

1 *A bleak setting can still be evocative.*

2 *Avoid sentimentality even when describing a place you love.*

3 *Use small details to build a sense of place.*

4 *Remember that your setting is a character in your book too.*

5 *Don't ever describe the dust as it floats through a beam of sunlight.*

12

Characterization

In this chapter you will learn:
- *how to create believable characters*
- *where to find your characters*
- *the importance of names*
- *how to develop your characters.*

When the characters are really alive before their author, the latter does nothing but follow them in their action, in their words, in the situation which they suggest to him.

Pirandello

Creating believable characters

The easiest mistake you can make when developing characters is to think that you can just put yourself and the people you know into a book. This is reckless because it can get you sued, but it is also a way of crippling yourself right from the start. Fiction is about making stuff up, including the people. A piece of fiction that is thinly disguised autobiography often fails on both counts. It fails to grip the way a fully realized story can, and fails to convince as autobiography should. Begun dishonestly the story will hit false notes all the way through and will prove an unsatisfactory read.

YOURSELF AS YOUR MODEL?

It is particularly unwise to use yourself as the sole model for your central character. This is because it is unlikely that you really know yourself well enough to produce a version that convinces in a book. Everyone's idea of themselves is wrong in so many ways. In fact, the proper job of a human being could be said to be getting to know yourself, and that is a lifetime's work. Writing novels might be part of that process, but making yourself the leading character in them probably isn't.

Insight

G. K. Chesterton put it well when he said, 'A good novel tells us the truth about its hero but a bad novel tells us the truth about its author.' (From *Heretics*)

Your characters are, of course, going to be based on people that you have met, and will include aspects of yourself. Mark Illis once wrote a novel where one of the narrators of the book is a girl we see grow from age 9 to 19. Mark wrote that book as a 40-year-old man and yet numerous readings at schools up and down the country have received enthusiastic endorsements from teenage girls thrilled to find stories that encapsulate what many of them experience. How does a 40-year-old man create a believable teenage girl? Mark stresses the similarities between himself and Rosa, the protagonist in *Tender*: 'There's a lot of me in her. Like her, I had a cool older brother. My parents were splitting up, just as hers are in the book. I wasn't gifted but I was considered very bright at school. I wasn't bullied but I did feel out of things; on the fringes of cliques rather than part of one particular group.' So why didn't he write Rosa as a boy?

'I enjoyed the challenge of making this character different from myself. That's part of the fun of writing fiction; you get to experience more lives than most people do.' In other words, in writing as a girl, Mark was forced to pay attention to the kind of things girls say and do. He had to stay alert and receptive in a way that he might not have done if the character had been based on himself. And of course he was free to have the young Rosa say and do things that the young Mark would never have done. Mark took aspects of his past self and then took liberties and risks. He played 'What if...' and 'Let's pretend...'.

LOVE YOUR MAIN CHARACTER

It is essential that you feel affection for your central character, even if no one else does. Jane Austen wrote of the clever but vain Emma Woodhouse, the eponymous heroine of *Emma*, 'I have written a heroine whom no one but me will love.' (The judgement of the author is not quite fair to poor Emma. She might be wilful, irritating, and not as bright as she thinks she is, but she is kindhearted and cheerful and, in the end, able to laugh at herself while learning from her mistakes.) So don't use your book to take vengeance on those who have crossed you. At least don't grant them the importance of making them central characters. Relegate your enemies to relatively unimportant parts of the story. That'll be far more wounding to them. One of the curious by-products of fiction writing is that people often want to see themselves in books, even if the characters they think most resemble them are distinctly unlikeable.

Your characters should have faults and weaknesses, but it is up to the readers to work these out. You are merely their guide. Readers want to be doing the principal legwork themselves. Like determined hikers, readers want to get to the summit under their own steam. They don't want to be carried. Your task as writer is to discreetly stop your readership drifting away from the paths that you want them to take. And, like a tour guide, you can't shape your readers' reactions to the sights they see as they progress through your story. They may pick up things that you haven't noticed and have very different feelings from you about the view from the top.

Insight

All stories are written twice: once by the writer and once by the reader. And your readers will have a different relationship from you to the characters you create. They may like some more, and others less.

Here is another of Martyn Bedford's exercises designed to help you create a believable character and to get right away from allowing your own personality to hog the limelight in your own story. You'll have a lot of fun with this.

Exercise 62

1 Note down a list of between five and ten words that you think might most accurately describe your main personality traits.
2 Beside these words write their opposites.
3 Using this second list, imagine yourself to be that person.
4 In that role, imagine that you are now applying for a place in the Big Brother house and write a video-diary monologue about yourself, saying why you should be allowed in.

Here's another exercise that builds on the work you did above.

Exercise 63

Imagine that a new person enters your life (e.g. a new neighbour, work colleague, classmate). Write in the first person about your first encounter with this person – either in the form of a short scene as might appear in a novel, or as an extended diary entry. While you should try to evoke the setting or context for this encounter – enabling the reader to visualize it – the focus should be on evocation of character. We should get an impression of this new person, and of the dynamics between you through your perceptions of this newcomer. Your reactions to this person will tell us a lot about you. The 'you' might be the real you, or an invented first-person narrator.

Stereotypes and archetypes

Lazy or unimaginative authors create stereotypes instead of living, breathing people. Obviously clichéd characters – the Scouse rascal, the hoodie-wearing teenage thug, the black gang member, the promiscuous and camp homosexual, the uptight bank manager – can be pernicious, pigeonholing certain groups and creating one-dimensional flat characters that won't inspire your readers to care. Archetypes are something different. Think back to fairy tales. There tends to be a stock cast to these stories: the beautiful princess (Cinderella, Sleeping Beauty, Rapunzel), usually blessed with talent and kindness as well as good looks; the handsome prince, brave, resourceful and determined; and the wicked stepmother, often a beauty herself but jealous of the younger princess and with magical qualities which she uses for bad ends. This is a basic triangle of characters where the wicked stepmother acts as a block between the desires of prince and princess. You can add to this basic cast. There is, for example, often a weak male authority figure (think of the woodcutter in Hansel and Gretel who doesn't stand up to his bullying wife when she explains that the children must be sent away). Think of the ugly sisters in Cinderella or the good fairies and bad fairies of many folktales, who help or hinder the protagonist.

Passed down through many generations of storytellers, and still told even to today's children at an early stage, these stories exert a powerful influence on our imaginations.

> **Insight**
> Your hero, flawed though he is, may well turn out to have many qualities of a fairytale prince. Your female protagonist may well have more than a touch of Cinderella about her. These archetypes can actually be helpful in creating powerful characters who will help your story move along in a compelling and dramatic way.

Exercise 64

1 *List the qualities of the major characters from a fairy tale you know well.*
2 *Now imagine characters with those qualities meeting in a modern setting, a school maybe or a hospital.*
3 *Rewrite the fairy tale for a modern audience using your new setting.*

Choosing names

It's hard for a character to live in your mind until you have found their name. Anyone who has named children (or even pets!) knows how important it is to get this right. Choosing a name is not a rational project but one that employs instinct and gut feeling. And when it comes to choosing fictional characters you have some additional problems. The names that you choose for villains shouldn't be libellous, i.e. the readers mustn't confuse Valerie Jones, the serial bigamist of your novel, with the real-life Valerie Jones who teaches piano in Bedford.

Neither must names detract from the action of the novel. They mustn't jar with the reader. I used to teach with a man called Mr Allcock. It's a perfectly respectable name but, as you can imagine, he got quite a lot of stick from teenage students. If I called a character Mr Allcock I would have to include some incidents where he had to deal with name-callers and that might hold up my plot. Also, readers being what they are, they would undoubtedly think that there was some reason I had given him so distinctive a moniker. Was he particularly testosterone-packed? Or was it an ironic comment on a lack of spirit? I don't want my readers' time to be taken up with irrelevancies like this. I want them to lose themselves in the action.

The master of fictional name-giving was Charles Dickens. Wackford Squeers, Nicholas Nickleby, Mr Micawber, Oliver Twist, Fagin, Sykes, Ebenezer Scrooge, Bob Cratchit, Mr Bumble, Uriah Heap: these are names which have passed into the general lexicon and some have become metaphors for a certain kind of person. Even children too young to read know what a Scrooge is. The names are rich, poetic and perhaps too ornamental for our more realistic times; yet Dickens himself declared that all the names were real, that he merely took them from directories of shopkeepers. Dickens is, of course, an unreliable narrator being a compulsive mythologist of his own life and work.

Insight

Many writers frequent graveyards in search of both names and unpleasant causes of death. Graveyards are also good for reminding yourself to crack on with the book. There may not be as much time to get it finished as you thought!

I wrote a lot of my last book sitting in a small library. From where I sat I could see both the prose and the poetry sections, and when I needed a new name I tended to choose the first name from a novelist and the surname from a poet.

One well-known contemporary novelist was alarmed and embarrassed when the kindly editor of her first book pointed out that the narrator's best friends included a Molly, a Polly and an Ollie, which gave a musical but comical note to interactions between them which she hadn't intended, and which even her agent hadn't noticed.

Names are important too for giving a flavour of the era in which you have set your story. A typical school register in an English school today may include Jacks, Alfies, Archies, Stanleys, Arthurs and Freds, as well as Mauds, Elsies and Millies, even maybe a Mabel, Reginald and a Wilfred! These old-fashioned names are really making a comeback and the novels of the future will no doubt have central characters whose names echo those of D. H. Lawrence. On the other hand there are some quite exotic names like Chakra, Zachery, Dieter, Daljit, Cottia and Romesh. There are precious few Steves or Pauls, names which were very common in the 1960s and 1970s. Meanwhile names like Niambh and Patrick, which were once only popular in Ireland – and Callum or Hamish similarly once just beloved of Scots – have entered the mainstream. Names go in and out of fashion and it is as well to be aware of some of these vagaries before you start calling your octogenarian great-grandmother character Chardonnay or Alisha.

Avoid having too many characters with similar names. We know that in real life there might be three Daves working in the warehouse, but your fictional warehouse had better have a variety of different names. You don't want to muddle a readership for whom life is too short to be working out which of the Daves is having an affair with the manager's wife, and which is the one who likes to do his allotment every Sunday without fail.

Insight

Good sources of names are www.babycentre.com, which provides lists of the top ten baby names for each state of the USA, and www.babynames.co.uk, which gives information on names in the UK. And then there is always the telephone directory. Or, as I said, the graveyard.

Describing your characters

It was once the convention to spend a long time describing characters. If you are a devotee of Victorian novels, you will know how pages can be taken up describing a character and their background. Nowadays we try and show character through action rather than tell the reader about it. A few phrases should be enough. Remember that the readers want to use their own imaginations while reading your book; that is, after all, the great pleasure of reading as opposed to watching television or films.

Read this description of Cordelia in *An Unsuitable Job for a Woman* by P. D. James.

> *Between their shoulders she could see her own reflection in the mirror behind the bar. Today's face looked no different from yesterday's face; thick, light brown hair framing features which looked as if a giant had placed a hand upon her head and the other on her chin and gently squeezed the face together; large eyes, browny-green under a deep fringe of hair; wide cheek bones; a gentle, childish mouth. A cat's face she thought, but calmly decorative among the reflection of coloured bottles and all the bright glitter of Mavis's bar.*

It is also important to weave your characterization into the development of the story as Ian McEwan has done in this extract from *The Cement Garden*.

> *That night my parents argued over the bags of cement. My mother, who was a quiet sort of person, was furious. She wanted my father to send the whole lot back. We had just finished supper. While my mother talked my father used a penknife to scrape black shards from the bowl of his pipe onto the food he had barely touched. He knew how to use his pipe against her. She was telling him how little money we had and that Tom would soon be needing new clothes for starting at school. He replaced the pipe between his teeth like a missing section of his own anatomy and interrupted to say that it was 'out of the question' sending the bags back and that was the end of it.*

It is often the most unusual details that are the most evocative. Everyone has their idiosyncrasies and you should be on the lookout for these, ready to incorporate them into your characters. These quirks of personality or movement are more likely to show up if you have your characters actively involved in the story rather than simply giving a general description.

Possessions

What people have, or what they aspire to, often says a great deal about them. We make snap judgements about people based on what they wear, but also on what else they own. Who hasn't browsed the bookshelves or music collection of a new acquaintance looking for clues to their character to emerge through their tastes? And a person who dreams of owning a vintage 2CV complete with a 'Nuclear Power No Thanks' sticker is likely to be a different kind of person from a Rolex-wearing BMW driver. Everything that people possess is the result of a distinct choice. Muesli or Coco Pops in the cupboard; full-fat or skimmed milk; black coffee or weak tea for breakfast; supermarket own-brand whisky or Laphroaig; trainers or handmade brogues; Armani or Oxfam; the Sex Pistols or Mahler; *Mad Men* or *Curb Your Enthusiasm*. And all the various possible choices in between.

Insight

In fiction, as in real life, first impressions last longest. And, just like real life, they can be wrong.

Characters can make inaccurate guesses about others based on the flimsy evidence of their possessions. Thinking about what your characters own can be a great way to make them become real, while their possessions may also give you a way of surprising your readers. Surprise is important because readers will be second-guessing you every step of the way, trying to work out the twists and turns of your plot. Your characters must remain believable, but they must also be capable of changing and of doing the unexpected, at least occasionally.

Exercise 65

1 *Write a list of 25 things that one of your characters might own. Don't spend too long thinking about it. Let your unconscious do at least some of the work here.*

(Contd)

2   *Now choose five of those items and write down how your character came by them.*
3   *Now choose one object that your character might prize above all the others and write a short scene describing what happens when that object goes missing.*

MORE THAN JUST OBJECTS

We all know that objects can have a powerful meaning for us. Most people cart boxes of artefacts from house to house, loft to loft, stuff that we can't bear to throw out though we haven't looked at any of it for years. Toys that we can't bear to part with or CDs we never play anymore but remind us of our youth. The kinds of objects our characters hang on to can become symbolic. Totems of their lives and personal belief-systems. They can show an alert reader a lot about them and what drives them.

Here is an exercise from the writer Phil Whitaker which really makes you think about the emotional resonance of objects. It is an exercise designed to explore the allusiveness of objects – the things we project on to them, the significance they hold for us – and it practises using this quality to communicate story and emotion to the reader.

Exercise 66

Your character is clearing junk out of the loft or garage. They come across an object from the past and decide to give it away (to a friend, a relation, a neighbour, a charity shop, etc.). Writing in the first or third person, create a history centred around the object. The scene should close with the handing over of the object. By the time this happens, the reader should understand the emotional significance of both the object and the decision to give it away.

Motive and desire

One of the things that will give your story momentum is deciding what your characters want from life. It might be more or better possessions, as outlined in the section above. It is more likely to be the things that that are represented by objects, i.e. power and status. Or it might be fame or love or security for the family. Some things your characters may not even be able to articulate. They may be subconscious, primeval urges: sweet old ladies can be driven by a sibling rivalry that started in infancy; a daughter may want her father's approval; a politician may be trying to make up for the fact that he had no power at school.

Insight

Subconscious drives are the essence of good dramas. It is worth thinking about what your characters most desire right at the beginning of any kind of story.

Whether they are striving to achieve their desires themselves, trying to protect their current position or responding to the actions of others, it is this response to deep drives and yearnings that will provide much of the impulse of your story. It is the constant struggle to resolve the deepest urges which will result in change in your characters. We've learned already that there can be no such thing as still life.

Insight

Change and growth is inevitable and necessary in fictional characters, just as it is in reality.

Exercise 67

For each of your major characters write down in very simple sentences what they want out of life. Write how they hope to achieve it but also what is stopping them achieving
(Contd)

it and what will happen if they can't get to where they want
to be. What will they do if they can't fulfil their dreams?

Of course achieving your desires can be just the start of some
serious trouble. Macbeth becomes king of Scotland but his life
spirals downwards from there. And the modern tabloid world is
littered with celebrity casualties unable to cope with getting what
they wished for.

Exercise 68

1 *Imagine that your central characters have achieved
   their desires. What is the worst thing that could happen
   to them as a result?*
2 *Write a short story that shows the unravelling of a life
   that should have been perfect.*

In the end, thinking about your characters 'off the page', outside of
the story itself, may help you move along faster when you do come
to write your novel. Here are three more short exercises that will
help you develop characters who will live on the page.

Exercise 69

Fill in a job application as your character, complete with
CV, education history, etc.

Exercise 70

Write an imaginary email correspondence between two of your favourite literary characters. Keep the total number of words to around 750.

Exercise 71

Travel with your character. As you go through your usual (non-writing) day, put yourself in your character's shoes – how would they see the school-run, the supermarket, work, etc? Have them react to the real-life situations around you. If they react just as you would have done then you are not trying hard enough and it's back to the drawing board.

Professional tip from Mavis Cheek

Characters are organic to your plot and all the best fiction is character led. When you have your story, you should know, in outline, who's going to be in it and what their function is. Details come later. For filling the character out there is no better place to observe human life than on a tube train or in a café. Just sit there and see who comes in and imagine what their inner life is – and how their outer appearance feeds those ideas of yours. But all mine come from out of my head. With bits and pieces of people I really know attached here and there.

Mavis Cheek is the author of many very successful novels including *Patrick Parker's Progress* and *The Sex Life of My Aunt* (Faber and Faber).

10 THINGS TO REMEMBER

1 *Your autobiography doesn't count as a novel.*

2 *Writing what you don't know – making things up – is part of the joy of writing fiction.*

3 *Fall in love with your main character (even if you think no one else will).*

4 *Use archetypes rather than stereotypes.*

5 *Make sure your characters have flaws and weaknesses.*

6 *Think hard about the names you give your characters.*

7 *Show character through action.*

8 *It is often the unusual details of a character that are the most evocative.*

9 *You can learn a lot about a character from the things they own.*

10 *Decide what your characters most desire from life, and the obstacles that are preventing them achieving their goals. This conflict is your story.*

13

Plotting

In this chapter you will learn:
- *about classic plots*
- *how to keep track of events*
- *the need to sacrifice your characters.*

Making books is a craft, like making clocks: it takes more than wit to be an author.

Jean de la Bruyère

The classic plots

In Chapter 10, I mentioned a little about plotting and gave you three basic storylines that are useful when first beginning. Now it's time to add to your armoury. Most people seem to agree that there are actually seven basic plots and that **all** stories are variations of these. This is a thesis developed by Christopher Booker in his influential work *The Seven Basic Plots: Why We Tell Stories* (Continuum Books, 2004). However, other writers identify a few more. Here are twelve templates which writers return to again and again.

1 **Killing the Dragon** – *whereby your hero or community faces a terrible threat and after a great struggle saves their family, community, or indeed the whole world from annihilation.*

2 **Rags to Riches** – *where the underdogs draw on inner qualities and triumph against all the odds.*

3 **The Quest or Journey** – *this is the heroic form we came across earlier where our heroes leave their home to find treasure. This doesn't have to be money, it could be a missing child, or a sacred object (remember King Arthur and the Holy Grail).*

4 **Voyage and Return** – *this is similar to the other heroic cycles mentioned earlier, where the protagonist leaves the life they know, their home, family and friends, in order to go to strange lands and returns via strange adventures.*

5 **Comedy** – *where confusion, misunderstandings and mutual incomprehension stop a character achieving their desires. This should turn out happily in the end.*

6 **Tragedy** – *whereby a character has some fatal flaw that undermines them as they struggle to achieve their goals. Despite all their qualities there is something within which stops the hero achieving. Or perhaps the goal was out of reach in the first place. Ultimately the hero overreaches. Think of Thomas Hardy's* Jude the Obscure *or* Macbeth.

7 **Rebirth** – *a character undergoes a complete transformation in order to get what they want.*

8 **Rite of Passage** – *the problems, traumas and painfully necessary learning experiences associated with growing up.*

9 **Rebellion** – *a character, community or group launches a struggle against authority.*

10 **The Switch** – *two characters swap lives.*

11 **The Faustian Pact** – *a character makes a bargain which they cannot get out of.*

12 **Rise and Fall** – *a character loses everything and must begin again from scratch. Often, despite everything, the protagonist succeeds in getting back to the top.*

Insight

It is natural to worry about originality, but these plots are as old as writing itself, and have been developed in a countless variety of ways. Whatever plot you use, it is your characters, your personal history, your style and thoughts that will make it unique.

Exercise 72

You have probably got quite a lot of ideas for stories in your notebook. Some of them will just be odd lines of overheard dialogue, or notes about a character you want to put into a story. Others will be a few words based around a theme. Still others will be more fully fleshed out than this. Try and pick out an idea and fit it to one of the basic plot ideas outlined on the previous pages. Try it on several of them. All of them even. You should find that each plot will turn your scrap of an idea into a quite new, but considerably more developed, story.

If you don't fancy trying out one of the classic plots try this exercise in plotting from the award-winning writer Sid Smith.

Exercise 73

Think of an interesting event, and then half a dozen possible explanations, e.g. a grave has been vandalized, and the reasons might be personal animosity because the dead wife is being buried with her husband and the vandal loved the wife... or the grave might have been vandalized because of racial prejudice... or... whatever.

When you have your explanations you actually have the plot of a detective story with a few false explanations, which your hero will have to investigate and see through to the true one.

Planning

Once you've got your central characters, your theme and your basic plot it is tempting to just start writing. For most people this is probably a mistake. It will be a lot easier if you think of your book as a series of scenes. Try and give yourself a scene breakdown in a similar way to those used by screenwriters. Then plan the beginning, middle and end of each scene. Aim to produce a one-page outline for each scene before you begin writing it. Try to think about what each character wants to get from the scene (not all characters will feature in every scene of course).

Creating a visual map will mean that you can make sure your characters are leading a properly chequered existence. If one character seems to be sailing pretty plainly through your book then you will need to create setbacks and disasters. Some characters must be rising as others are falling and if these vicissitudes can be tracked at a glance, you will find that you stay focused.

Having a clear and colourful plan (buy lots of marker pens or felt tips!) will also help you as your characters move towards a climax. If you put this climax down on your map, then it gives you an end point. Tension should build in your story. There is a sense in which all books should be thrillers.

There is something too about having a physical connection with your book. It might be that you are one of the few writers left who work with a pen, but the chances are that you prefer to use a PC. Handwriting is essentially making pictures and utilizes a different area of the brain from that used for working with a keyboard. The physical effort involved in handwriting gives you a bodily involvement with it. I'm not arguing that you should jettison your laptop, but I do think that having a large, colourful concrete object that you have worked on physically, that represents your overall scheme, gives you a special kind of clarity towards your project.

Suspense

A lot of new writers give away everything about the plot and the characters in the opening chapter. You can give a lot less information than you might expect. On the other hand, objects and people mentioned early should return later. Nothing should be wasted. You are going to need to resolve all the journeys which the characters embark on. This is another argument in favour of your colourful wallchart. You should be able to see at a glance where your characters have got to.

Insight

Suspense is the art of not answering readers' questions. You are delaying gratification in order that they have a more satisfactory pay-off later on. You are also giving readers the pleasure of writing the book along with you. You are making them work, and readers – masochists that they are – enjoy that. Writing a book is always a collaborative act between you and your readers. You have to give them room to contribute.

Where did I put those keys?

One thing you should do as you plan your book is think about where to put the objects. We've said already how important objects can be, not just in revealing character, but in creating symbols for your theme.

In order to add richness to your novel, keep note of any object that appears in chapter one and plot where it is at any given moment in your book. Obviously you might not mention that object much but if you know where it is you are able to call upon it when you need to. There should be certain 'sacred' objects that return at vital parts of the story. It might be a book the character was reading in the first chapter, a pen or an item of clothing. It might even be a bunch of keys. In a way it doesn't even matter if they are important to the plot, but knowing where your things are as well as your people can help develop a richer book – if only because it makes you focus on it twice as hard.

Exercise 74

Imagine that you are inventing a treasure hunt based upon your story. Draw out a map of the plot; now imagine that you have to bury significant objects at key moments. What objects would they be? Whom would they belong to?

Writer as sadist

You are going to have to be mean to your characters. Even the ones you like. In fact, especially the ones you like. Your characters must labour under the burdens of problems to start with, and these should get worse before they get better. And even when they get better this should often prove to be a false dawn. You have to treat your characters mean in order to keep your readers keen.

You'll need to keep a ready eye out for stories of the kind that can fall – like rain – into a person's life.

Insight
Sad but true: an interest in human disasters and frailty is essential in a novelist.

MURDERING YOUR BABIES

Writing is a brutal job. It's exhausting, frustrating, upsetting. And one of the most upsetting things about it can be the need to kill off your characters. Sometimes in order to move things along you are going to have to make dramatic, surprising and risky decisions. Somewhere along the line there will come a point when you have to sacrifice a favourite son. And by sacrifice, I really do mean 'kill'. Novels are worlds where the same stuff happens as happens in any world. Births, marriages, love, sex, work and friendship, but also divorce, disease, accidents, death and crime.

Insight
Readers want chills as well as thrills and part of your job is to give those to them.

But there is another, perhaps better, reason for killing off some of your favourite characters. It can free you up. Just as some widows and widowers blossom after the death of a partner, however beloved that partner was – developing new skills and interests that surprise those who knew them before – so you as a novelist might be liberated by having to allow some of the other characters to work harder.

We're not advocating killing off your hero early on. That seems foolhardy. Getting rid of a hero in whom your readers have invested significant emotional capital seems a reckless and difficult trick to pull off. But there may be a secondary character who can threaten to unbalance a book, who just takes up too much damn room. Getting rid of them might provide a surprising twist but also allow a period of calm and reflection, after which those characters that are left can assume control of the story.

Insight
Being forced from your comfort zone into the company of characters you feel less at ease with may well benefit your book as a whole.

We'll come to murdering your babies again in a less literal sense when we talk about style and its many enemies in Chapter 15.

Subplots

A subplot is a story that echoes or contrasts with the central narrative of your book. It may well involve minor characters in more central positions. Imagine that you have a story where a domineering husband leaves the family home to go and fight in a war. Your major plot might concern itself with his wife becoming independent as she starts to do the things that he did before. Perhaps she gets a job, or starts meeting other men, or discovers other possibilities in her life. She starts to grow, develop and change. It is a difficult time for the country but a liberating time for her. A subplot might concern itself with the relationships her children build up while their mother is working and their father is away. Perhaps they develop an unexpected rapport with the father's mother which will cause conflict later in the book when the father returns from fighting and expects everything to be the same as it was when he left.

Your subplot needs to be satisfying in itself but you don't want it to overwhelm the action. Remember that the theme of your subplot will work best if it is a different – perhaps very different – take on the theme of your book as a whole.

Insight
Subplots provide satisfying diversions away from the main action while at the same time giving the reader another oblique perspective on it. They also heighten the suspense by taking the narrative in a new direction just as the reader felt they were going to get some resolution.

We have spent a long time considering different methods of planning a novel. Some writers hardly plan at all. John Fowles said, 'I begin with an image, a ghost of an idea, nothing more, not knowing where it will lead.' Iris Murdoch, on the other hand, planned everything in great detail. Most novelists fall somewhere between these two positions. As a novelist I tend to have a loose plan based around my ghost of an idea, but I fully expect it to change as I progress and as the characters begin to seize control. I then wrest control back in the redrafts before eventually letting my characters do what they are compelled to do in the end. However, I am still learning as a writer and I hope my techniques will become varied as I progress. Perhaps my next book will be one where I plan absolutely every detail. And maybe the one after that will be the one where I start with just a title and nothing else.

Insight

Whatever kind of writer you are, the less planning you do before your first draft, the more extensive your rewrites will be.

Endings

Anyone can start a novel, but keeping going and completing it is the preserve of the dedicated. You have to decide what kind of ending you want. Just as in a short story, you have the option of a closed ending, where everything is tied up, or an open ending where the possibilities for the characters stretch out into a future that is unwritten, except in the mind of the reader who has just finished the story. You want to avoid the reader thinking 'so what?' They have invested a good chunk of time and emotional energy into the book and they want to feel richly compensated for this. They want a return.

So how do you know when to finally give readers what they crave? Essentially your characters will tell you. When they have solved their major problems and moved on, ready to start a new phase in life, that's when you should stop too.

Insight

Beginnings are easy. Endings are hard.

Here are another two exercises from the great Martyn Bedford that allow you to test just how far you have come in beginning to think seriously about your novel.

Exercise 75

Select an incident from your childhood and write it as a brief scene (you may be faithful to the actual incident or you may fictionalize). You are free to write it from the child's perspective, or from that of another participant or witness, and to choose either of the narrative viewpoints (i.e. first or third person). Pay attention to feelings and emotion as well as to dialogue, description and action – the purpose is to combine place/setting, characterization and event/situation in one short piece of prose.

Exercise 76

Invent a story that includes all of the following: a schoolboy; an old lady (characters); a ten pound note (object); a railway station (place); loneliness (emotion).

Professional tip from Christopher Wakling

Plot is causality. It's the why of the journey, not the where. It's the reason for the detours, not the detours themselves. This happened, and then that happened, and then this happened too: that's not a plot, it's a sequence of events. This happened which made that happen, and so that happened as well – that's plot. Plot makes things happen.

Christopher Wakling is the author of four novels including *Beneath The Diamond Sky* and *Undertow* (Picador).

10 THINGS TO REMEMBER

1 *Plots are not just a series of events.*

2 *Plots make things happen.*

3 *There is no such thing as a wholly original plot.*

4 *Keep a visual chart of the progress of your main characters.*

5 *Your book is a partnership between you and your readers. Make them do some of the work.*

6 *Keep track of the 'sacred objects' in your book.*

7 *Be mean to your characters. Especially the ones you like.*

8 *Subplots provide an interesting counterpoint to your main narrative drive.*

9 *The less planning you do before you begin, the more redrafting you will have to do when you finish.*

10 *Anyone can start a story. It takes real skill to finish one.*

14

Dialogue

In this chapter you will learn:
- *the difference between real speech and dialogue*
- *how to present dialogue on the page*
- *how to ensure your dialogue relates to the story context.*

I see people in terms of dialogue and I believe that people are their talk.

Roddy Doyle

Life versus art

Alice (in Wonderland) wondered, 'What is the use of a book without pictures or conversation?' And she's got a point. The conversation in your fiction is hugely important in helping give your story pace and sparkle. Dialogue in fiction is used to convey information, to move the plot and to provide us with a richer understanding of the characters. But what you can't do in fiction is simply write speech as it occurs in real life. Students new to writing often defend tedious dialogue with the defence that they copied it down verbatim from an exchange they heard on a bus or in a café. But if you are going to write speech exactly as it occurs in normal human discourse then you are going to have a very long, very boring book.

People speaking to one another 'er' and 'um' and lose track of what they were saying, and digress and interrupt one another and get distracted. They repeat themselves, they hesitate, repeat themselves again and often go on and on and on and on and on and... you get the picture.

Insight

The paradoxical thing about writing believable dialogue is that you have to get rid of the very things which make it real. Real speech would be hugely complicated to reproduce on the page and would give your reader a migraine.

Dialogue in a book is there to fulfil two functions: it must move the story forward and it must allow us to get to know the characters better. If it is not doing this then it is not needed. So keep dialogue short and to the point. Pare it down wherever possible. On the other hand, careful use of speech can save you writing lots of unnecessary description.

A sentence like: 'Hey Judy, like that top. Very swirly. And pink. Very you.' stops you having to spend ages describing Judy's clothes, and also tells you something about both characters (i.e. Judy likes wearing colourful eccentric clothes and whoever is speaking to her is a patronizing old bag, or maybe just doesn't like her very much). Whatever the case, there's quite a lot going on behind one fairly innocuous line of dialogue.

Exposition

Too much information in speech will make the character sound stilted and false. As a general rule try to keep a character's lines of dialogue to no more than three uninterrupted sentences at a time. This is a rule you can break occasionally (if you have a long-winded character, or when someone finally spills out words they have been storing up for a long time), but a novel is not really the place for monologues or for wordy exchanges of views.

Conversations in books should not be like televised political debates where each person gets sufficient airtime to set out a balanced, logical case. (Sadly, too many are.)

Exercise 77

1 *Record five minutes of two of your family or friends speaking.*
2 *Write out a verbatim transcript.*
3 *Now rewrite the exchange as though it was a passage in a novel, cutting what you feel is unnecessary and keeping what might move a story on or tell us about character.*

He said, she said

New writers are often seduced into thinking that they should come up with alternatives to 'he said' and 'she said'. The results are always clunky and often comically archaic. Think of this little exchange for example:

> *'What on Earth is going on?' demanded Julian.*
> *'Julie's gone mad.' exclaimed Sophie.*
> *'I must have Walter or I'll die.' protested Julie.*
> *'That man again!' Julian ejaculated. 'Over my dead body.'*

Ridiculous isn't it? It's only amateur writers who feel the need to find constant alternatives to he said/she said. Most established writers use this phrase without it intruding at all, whereas the alternatives always muddy the flow of the text, making it far more awkward than it need be. Often you don't need any attributive verb like 'he said' at all, merely the speech itself, followed by the next one.

The best way to discover whether or not your dialogue is
working is to read it aloud.

Mastering voices

Each character should have a distinctive way of speaking. The
way someone talks, the grammar, the choice of vocabulary: all of
this tells us a lot about them. We learn about social class, about
education, about the way they see the world and the way they see
themselves from these kinds of clues. Everyone has a unique way
of using language and you must be careful that your characters
don't bleed into each other.

DIALECTS

Don't be tempted to resolve this problem by using dialect.
Obviously a Cockney cabbie must sound like a Cockney cabbie,
but do this by his turns of phrase rather than by using apostrophes
to replace his missing 'h's. This will be easier to do when you are
writing about people and communities familiar to you.

'BAD' LANGUAGE

I have had more complaints about my tendency towards what my
Yorkshire friends call 'Effing and Jeffing' than for anything else.
This is particularly true of pieces that I have written for the stage.
I don't make any apology for this. Swearing is used as punctuation
by whole swathes of people now, and not just underclass characters
either. In fact no one swears quite like the upper classes. In terms
of imaginative vulgarity, a graduate of Cheltenham Ladies' College
can hold her own with any docker or squaddie.

Sometimes it's hardly believable if characters *don't* use four-letter
words. You should use language truthfully. However, unthinking
repetition of profanity, when not used for effect, can grow very
tiresome very quickly. You should be aware too that words when

printed are much louder than when spoken. I hardly notice when the plumber who lives next door swears. He does it so often it's like breathing. But if he was to swear in a letter or email to me, then I'd be quite shocked.

See John Cooper Clarke's fantastic poem 'Evidently Chickentown' to see how repetition of a particular swearword (when nicely done!) can be used with devastating brilliance.

Be mindful though that this might also be an area where you might have to compromise with a publisher or editor.

Context

It is important that your reader knows where the conversations are taking place. You don't need to labour the point, but some action to help the reader see the scene is always helpful.

If a vicious argument is taking place in the kitchen, then there are a whole host of actions that the characters might do which might help reveal the way their emotions are moving as the row progresses. Rummaging in the fridge or determinedly making tea as a wife confesses to an affair might show a man trying to hold on to normality or maintain dignity as his world falls apart. Cleaning the floor or getting the kids' tea ready while a husband rambles on about his day at the office can be done in such a way as to show boredom, exasperation, repressed dislike, as can that same wife's non-committal monosyllabic interjections to her husband's talk.

The point is that conversations happen in a setting that the reader wants to be able to picture.

Layout

For layout on the page, study good modern writing and note that a new paragraph is required each time a different character speaks. Action by a character who has just spoken or who is about to speak appears on the same line.

Single inverted commas are usually employed for dialogue, with double ones for quotes within a speech (e.g. 'I saw "The Three Sisters" at our local theatre last week.'), but publishers have their own preference and sometimes this procedure is reversed.

Some publishers use dashes. Others use no speech indications at all but make it obvious in the text nevertheless. Look at this example:

> *Get away from me, you ape. Still he comes nearer. I can feel his hot breath close to my cheek. You stink. Go away.*
>
> *That's not very nice, he says. He's trying to smile but it's not really working. I'm not very nice, I say. If I just keep him away from me till Dan arrives. Dan is my boyfriend.*

You see how you can still tell who's talking? If you read enough books you'll find a contemporary style that you feel happy adopting.

Thoughts should never be put into inverted commas. It's too easy to confuse them with speech. A good technique is to begin the thought with a capital letter: 'She thought, He's no idea what I'm driving at'. You might prefer a colon to a comma after

'She thought'. A good guide to all these punctuation and layout dilemmas is Lynne Truss's *Eats, Shoots and Leaves*.

Exercise 78

Write 500 words of dialogue in which two people engage in a violent quarrel. Do it in the form of a play first, with only the two names, the words spoken, and one line to set the scene. Then rewrite with action and setting sketched in, but still keep the length of the overall piece to 500 words.

Professional tip from Eleanor Moran

Dialogue is as much about what your character doesn't say as what they do. You must think about how they express themselves in a way that is unique to them.

Eleanor Moran is the author of *Stick or Twist* (Michael Joseph).

10 THINGS TO REMEMBER

1 *Dialogue in a novel doesn't simply repeat everyday speech.*

2 *Dialogue must move a story forward.*

3 *Dialogue should allow us to get to know characters better.*

4 *A novel is not the place for monologues.*

5 *Alternatives to he said/she said can make a text seem awkward.*

6 *Read your dialogue aloud.*

7 *Each character should have a distinct way of speaking.*

8 *Keep swearing to a minimum.*

9 *Thoughts should never be put into inverted commas. They are not speech.*

10 *Avoid writing dialect phonetically.*

15

The difficult business of second drafts

In this chapter you will learn:
* *how to revise and edit your work*
* *how to enable your true voice to shine through*
* *the importance of good grammar and punctuation.*

Of every four words I write, I strike out three.

Nicolas Boileau

The craft of revision

All writing is rewriting. No one ever has handed in a first draft, posted it off and sat back to receive the applause and the cheques.

'First drafts are shit' said Hemingway, but he should have added that they are necessary shit. I'm a real believer in pouring out a first draft, leaving it to compost for a while and then going over it systematically and ruthlessly. Be your own harshest critic.
The chances are that you'll need to revise everything. If you've left enough time between drafts, new and better ideas will have occurred to you already. You'll have accrued new material, much of it deserving of a place in the final text. This is good, because there will also be plenty from the first draft that needs cutting.

When you embark on the rewriting process the first thing is to read your work very carefully. You'll need to know your novel inside out. And don't read it on the computer. Make sure you have a hard copy printed double-spaced with a wide margin, so that you can scribble notes and revise phrases. There is something about having real paper in your hand that enables you to spot mistakes much, much more easily than when they are on the screen. New ideas will occur to you all the time as you read your manuscript and I promise that the craft of revision, which seemed so painful when you began, will quickly begin to create its own exhilarating energy. When you first contemplate revising a book it can seem like climbing the same hard, high mountain all over again without even the thrill of conquering it to look forward to. You've already seen the view from the summit, you've already had the triumphant glow of having achieved the top. Surely doing it again just gives you the slog without the joy? Fortunately, though there are numerous similarities between writing and mountain-climbing, they are not an exact match.

As you progress through your redraft you will find new routes, new views, new and better ways to express yourself. Your copy of your text will become covered in scribbles and crossings out and hieroglyphs that will mean nothing to you but are your blueprint for the book you were always meant to write.

There will also be times when you smile at your work.

When not to murder your babies

In 1914 in *On the Art of Writing*, Sir Arthur Quiller-Couch wrote:

> *Whenever you feel an impulse to perpetrate a piece of exceptionally fine writing, obey it – wholeheartedly – and delete it before sending your manuscript to press. Murder your darlings.*

This is crazy, isn't it? Joe Orton said that whenever he came across a piece in his own work that made him laugh out loud, then that is what he would end up cutting. More fool him. Writing is so often difficult and painful that it seems perverse to make it harder than it needs to be. You started writing because there were things only you could say. And because you felt you had a unique way of saying them. Why cut what makes your work special? Why stop doing the thing that you do best? No one thought it was a good idea to put George Best in goal; no one puts the marathon runner Paula Radcliffe in for the 100-metre sprint. Of course we have to be alert for work that seems pretentious. And some of your work which seems especially fine on a first or second reading will seem awkward in a third draft when everything around it has changed. But in this context *don't* kill your babies, nurture them, work on them, improve on them. These stylistic tics may be the very things future readers cherish about your work.

Exercise 79

Give yourself a tick every time you come across something in your work that you really really like. Don't cheat, you have to genuinely love it. Then count your ticks. Do the same exercise after a redraft; with any luck the number has gone up significantly. You are doing this as a confidence boost. You are a good writer, stick at it.

Working preferences

We suggested that you write in scenes, and you should revise the same way. Does every scene deserve its place in the piece as a whole and does each sentence within the scene need to be there?

Some writers feel the need to perfect each sentence as far as possible before going on to the next. This is fine. Many of the best writers work this way. I don't. I believe in roughing the work out in full and going back. Others will write out a thousand words in rough in the morning and then edit and revise those words in the afternoon. There are nearly as many working methods as there are writers and there's certainly no right way to go about it. However, you should beware of honing one particular area of your work so much that it holds you up and you never finish. That's the literary equivalent of pruning your hanging baskets while the garden quietly turns into a jungle.

A lot of new writers have a fantastically polished first chapter and struggle to complete the whole book. Good enough is sometimes good enough.

Insight
Perfectionism can simply be fear of failure in a nicer frock.
It can be a hindrance. Don't get it right. Get it written.

What all writers should be wary of is just revising on the computer screen. The edit tools are very seductive. The urge to spend all day cutting, pasting and rearranging the text can get in the way of actually doing any writing. It is easy to convince yourself that you are writing when you are in fact simply typing.

Points for revision

1. HAVE YOU BEGUN IN THE RIGHT PLACE?

A lot of novice writers find themselves apologizing to those kind people who have volunteered to be the first readers of

a work – 'The story doesn't really get going until chapter three'
they stammer. In which case, chapter three should actually be
the first chapter. Amazingly, similar apologies crop up in the
covering letters sent with submissions to agents and publishers.

There is also that tendency among new writers to give too
much away in the first chapter. However, you should aim to grab
the reader in the opening passages, whatever genre you are
writing in.

2. IS THERE TOO MUCH BACK STORY?

There might well be information about your characters that you
need to know but the reader doesn't. We have considered many
different ways of creating fully rounded characters, but some of
this should inform you as you write, rather than be for the reader
to plough through.

3. ARE THERE ANY UNINTENTIONAL REPETITIONS?

The answer is almost certainly yes. When you are writing at speed
and in the heat of inspiration, this is understandable. So revise with
care, eliminating all the words which could undermine the flow of
your prose. A more difficult problem to eradicate might be where
you have repeated ideas rather than phrases. It is easy to say the
same thing twice, in different ways.

4. IS ANYTHING IRRELEVANT?

Have you included material which is not related to your central
theme? The first draft of my first book certainly included a
great deal that had personal resonance for me, but which was
unnecessary in terms of my plot. It all had to go.

5. IS YOUR RESEARCH SHOWING?

This is a particular danger for non-fiction writers, but novelists can
suffer from it too. As you get ready to write a book your reading

and trawling through the weirder, wilder reaches of Google will have unearthed all sorts of arcane facts that you'll be tempted to crowbar into your book. Don't. Stories are wiry, tough creatures but they can still be crushed beneath a weight of unnecessary research. Your reader may become frustrated trying to wade through the maze you have created for them. They may give up. The trivial pursuits champion at a dinner party, who knows a million facts about every subject that comes up in conversation, may be nice, clever and widely read, yet also unlikely to ever get a girlfriend. In the same way your book too may find itself a wallflower in the library through inflicting too much unnecessary knowledge upon the reader.

6. IS THERE ANY DEAD WOOD?

One writer I know sets his students this exercise: they must write for 30 minutes on a set subject and then they must cut every other word. Sometimes the result is gobbledygook, but often individual sentences and paragraphs are improved in surprising ways. Cutting the dead wood is the very essence of good writing. Get rid of whatever is superfluous. Slash and burn. Be ruthless. My hard drive contains 100,000 words of my first book that were never used. The result of four complete drafts. And how do you spot the dead wood? If you have let your manuscript simmer in a drawer, away from prying eyes and sunlight for a good long while, then dead wood will leap out at you. More dead wood will become apparent if you read the work out loud. Also, every sentence over 30 words is almost certainly too long.

If you have spent as much time on revising as you did on writing the book in the first place, you might be tempted to think that *now* it is finished. It must be. Well, put it away for another few days and come back to it again. There will still be too many words. And when your candid friends have given it the once over, there will still be more to cut.

There will still be material that embarrasses you whenever you think of it.

The art of good style

The point of getting rid of all the clutter is to highlight your style,
not to obscure it. If you write in your own way, and do it regularly,
you will establish a style which you feel comfortable with. Cutting
will be part of the process of clearing all that doesn't fit with your
style or your strategy.

STUDY EXCELLENCE

One of the great things about becoming a serious writer is that
you become a very serious reader. Every book you read from now
on will have lessons for you; every facet of that book will have
heightened resonance for you. Reading will still be an enjoyable
entertainment, but it will be more than that.

Every author will be a tutor, every story a guide for your own
work. This is not to say that you should copy other writers, though
actually of course you should. Sometimes writers say that they
don't read while they are writing in case another writer's style
rubs off. To me that would seem to be the point.

Guitarists watch the hands of other players in order to spot new
chord shapes and tricks of technique. Artists can become incredibly
learned about the techniques of creating colour from the eighteenth
century. Knowing all you can about your chosen craft gives you
more options in your own writing. You should stay open-minded
to writers whose taste is not your own, whose politics are not
your own, whose subject matter you might find distasteful. You
don't need to be a lesbian to enjoy the strong characters, heady

atmospherics and powerfully plotted novels of Sarah Waters, for example.

You should also read contemporary work wherever possible. The world has moved on since the books you studied in high school. If you are serious about writing you need to know what is happening now, as well as the masters of the past. Literature is a fashion-conscious business just like any other, and tastes change.

Everyone should have read *Treasure Island* at least three times, just as everyone should read Raymond Carver, Charles Dickens, Edgar Allan Poe, J. D. Salinger, Graham Greene, Jane Austen, P. D. James, George Macdonald Fraser's *Flashman* stories and F. Scott Fitzgerald. But you should also read E. L. Doctorow, A. L. Kennedy, Suzanne Berne, Don DeLillo, Anne Tyler, Deborah Levy, Sarah Hall, D. B. C. Pierre, Martin Amis and Monica Ali. All modern, all very different in approach, all master storytellers as well as great stylists. Keep an eye on the present, weigh up the competition and remember not to be depressed by great writing – just reading it with attention is building up your own literary muscle – but remember too that thinking you could do better is also a legitimate motivation for your own work.

Insight

Writers choose their own mentors. Anyone still in print or still available on the shelves of a library is there to help guide you towards expressing yourself clearly and well. To help you find your own voice.

The enemies of good style

CLICHÉ

A cliché is a phrase that has become stale with overuse: 'weak at the knees', 'over the moon', 'white as a sheet'. As *The New Fowler's Modern English Usage* reminds us, the word cliché has 'come to be applied to commonplace things of other kinds – visual images, stock situations, remarks in radio and television (and now, if you'll excuse me I've got work to do), ideas and attitudes etc'.

You should also avoid clichéd situations: the husband who arrives home from work unexpectedly to find his wife in the arms of another man; the suicide note on the mantelpiece. Dianne Doubtfire put it well when she said, 'Good style has a lot to do with freshness of vision.' My personal pet hate among clichés is where someone seems to vomit noisily as they come across a dead body. I'm sure this happens sometimes, but in literature, theatre and television it happens all the time and in the same kind of ways.

SENTIMENTALITY

This is normally caused by over-writing a powerful scene which involves a character you care for. It's easily done when that character is facing a moment of acute crisis. Read these passages with a stony heart, and be particularly receptive to criticisms that any early readers may have about these passages. As Carl Jung put it, 'Sentimentality is a superstructure covering brutality.'

CLUMSY PHRASES

These are phrases which can jerk readers from the world you are constructing for them into the real world. Something irritates. Reading out loud any phrases you suspect might be awkward will be the final test. Speaking the words out loud will also help you find your way to a better way of putting things.

TOO MANY ADJECTIVES AND ADVERBS

The most common, but most easily corrected of all the mistakes beginners make, is to overuse adjectives and adverbs. Adverbs also tend to be the mark of lazy writing, telling us what someone thinks or feels rather than showing us. Adjectives have a dulling effect on a piece of prose, limiting the reader's own imagination and suggesting a lack of confidence on the part of the writer.

It engenders a feeling that they can't quite manage to describe a person or event properly. It makes readers feel that they are not in safe hands: that the pilot doesn't quite know how to fly the plane.

Insight

Getting rid of as many adverbs as you can when revising a piece of work will be the simplest way to improve it.

Exercise 80

Write a descriptive piece of 300 words or so, using no adjectives or adverbs. When the work is finished you may add one of each.

Exercise 81

Now imagine that you have been asked to turn that 300-word description into a 200-word piece for an anthology of new writing.

POOR PUNCTUATION

It's not really the role of this book to teach you about punctuation – for that you need Lynne Truss's excellent *Eats, Shoots and Leaves* – but you should be aware that editors will not correct incoherent grammar or punctuation, they will merely assume that you don't know what you're doing. In particular, be careful to use colons and semicolons correctly.

The other important point to make about punctuation (which is also actually a style point) is to refrain from using exclamation marks. It is like adding boom-boom after a joke. OK if you're Basil Brush but unacceptable otherwise.

Insight

Contrary to popular opinion, publishers still expect their writers to be able to sort out their own punctuation and spelling. They won't have anyone who will do it for you. If your manuscript suggests that its writer is illiterate it will go in the bin.

Professional tip from Monique Roffey

When you come to do a second draft, that's the time to ask yourself if the narrative devices you've chosen, perhaps instinctively, are the right ones to use – tense, point of view, systems of images, metaphors and language too. Are these devices working, and have you been consistent? These are the big questions to consider once the first draft is over. After that, take a week off to sit in bed with jugs of coffee and READ the manuscript; by that I mean skim-read at least twice – for a bird's eye view of the plot and the overall structure.

Once you are happy you are telling the story in the right way, read the whole thing much more carefully – and start to make notes for changes and cuts. Once that is done, apply notes.

Monique Roffey is the author of *Sun Dog* (Scribner).

10 THINGS TO REMEMBER

1 *All good writing is rewriting.*

2 *Be ruthless.*

3 *Revise on a hard copy rather than on a screen.*

4 *Reward yourself when you find something good.*

5 *Nurture your quirks and idiosyncrasies.*

6 *Good enough sometimes really is good enough.*

7 *Your readers don't need to know everything about a character. You do. They don't.*

8 *Don't let your research show.*

9 *Study excellence.*

10 *No one else will sort out your grammar, spelling and punctuation for you.*

16

Writing stage plays

In this chapter you will learn:
- *ways to create characters for the stage*
- *how to write stage dialogue*
- *about the need for action and conflict*
- *how to structure and market a play.*

This is what I tell them about drama.
A stranger comes to the door
And the arranged plates fall off the walls.

Iain Crichton Smith 'Drama Workshop'

The purpose of theatre

The play is increasingly becoming a marginal art form. Fewer and fewer people go and see plays and hardly anyone at all is brave enough to go and see a new play by a new writer with an unknown lead. When was the last time you went to see one?

The reasons are not hard to find. Plays are expensive. It can cost £20 ($30) or more for a ticket, so with drinks, programmes, a meal out and a babysitter an average couple can have spent a substantial amount to spend two hours trapped in a stuffy black box with no escape route should the play not prove to their taste. It's a hard expense to justify – even for the most dedicated lover of the arts. And yet... and yet... the theatre continues to survive and to throw up some outstanding, incredible work. Some of which even makes money occasionally.

It can be a hugely exciting medium. It is, after all, one of the few experiences that can't be downloaded. In live performance, there is always a sense of danger present, an immediacy that can't be found anywhere else. When great actors are performing great work, directed imaginatively on a stunning set, there is simply nothing else that can exhilarate in quite the same way. A good night at the theatre has some of the thrill of attending a top live sporting event. It is an experience that is individual – we all experience the ideas and action of the play in our own way – but it is also communal. All of us in the audience have come together to share our common humanity. Part of us is lost to the crowd. An audience has its own dynamic which is greater than, and different from, all the individuals in it. It is an intimate, very powerful place to be.

Insight

The first thing to say to any prospective theatre writer is to remind them to get out there and see some new plays. Don't rely on what you remember from school visits long ago. Theatre has changed and is throwing up some of the most provocative, challenging and mesmerizing work.

Exercise 82

Make four columns. In the first write a list of the last five plays you went to see and the rough dates. In the second give them a star rating out of five. Five stars for amazing, one for unwatchable. (Writers, directors and actors hate the star rating system adopted by most reviewers, mainly because it is all readers of reviews look at. I can totally understand this frustration. Nevertheless, I think we can all agree that it is a very useful shorthand guide for audiences.) In the third column write a couple of words or a sentence

(Contd)

saying why you went to the show. If it was because of a
star name write 'star', if it was because of a review put that
down. If it was because a friend told you it was good then
put that down. In the final column write down one thing
that stood out from the play. If it was a line, or a speech,
then jot that down, but it might also be the set, the costumes
or just one piece of action that stayed with you.

At the end of this exercise you should have a clear idea of how
hard it is to get people to the theatre, what does attract them
and also that what captures the imagination is not necessarily
the words.

It should also be clear to you that if you haven't seen a good play
in a while, then you need to get out more. Find the listings pages
in your local paper or on the web and book some tickets. Most
theatres now have special deals available for those who book
early or who book several shows at once, or who will see the
matinee or who are prepared to go on unpopular nights and sit
in the cheapest seats.

Stage characters

Characters are vital in a play. They can be extreme, but they should
be three-dimensional. They should have vitality. And they should
not be your ciphers. They should think, breathe, walk and talk
for themselves. Yes, you gave them life but you shouldn't think
that gives you the right to push them around and tell them what
to do, any more than you can completely control the lives of your
children or friends.

You may not be able to control the directions which your
characters move in, or the places where they lead you, but you
will still need to know everything about them. Where they went to

school, their first romances, their job, what they like for breakfast, whether they prefer coffee to tea. Everything. Your audience doesn't need to know this, but you do.

We've already done a lot of work on finding characters and you should have a little store built up and developed from those that you see around you every day, or that you used to know well. People who, with a little imaginative work, could change from ordinary real-life workmates, family, friends and acquaintances into characters given life by you.

What you should not do is create a character who is too obviously heroic. A kind of superman. They won't be believable. They may even be ridiculous and that ridiculousness will be heightened if they are the character that is meant to be most like you.

Insight

Your characters should be real, flawed human beings. And that remains true if your subject is Mother Teresa or Pope John Paul II or Gandhi. Perhaps even more so.

Exercise 83

Choose three characters for this exercise: make one older and one younger and the third can be whatever age you want. It doesn't matter what sex they are. Make sure you give them a name; names are very important. It is hard to make a character come alive until you've found the right name for them.

Set your clock, watch or phone for 15 minutes and simply brainstorm as many questions as you can that you might want to ask your characters. These might range from 'What is your address?' all the way to 'Do you believe in God?'

Now spend some more thoughtful time making sure that you get all your characters' answers to the questions. At the end of this exercise you should have a more complete idea of what makes them tick. You should know them better as complex, fully rounded human beings.

Insight

Small casts are a good idea. You don't need many characters for a decent play. These days, with the economics of the business being what they are, the fewer actors a producer needs to employ, the more interest they may have in reading your piece.

It is helpful if your characters are very different from one another. Now you need to find a reason for your characters to meet and begin their journey together. You need an inciting incident.

The inciting incident

This is the thing that kicks off the play. The thing that brings your characters together. Some kind of event. And it is striking how often in plays this is actually the *aftermath* of something major. *Macbeth* starts just after the battle where Macbeth and King Duncan have seen off the rebel Macdonald and his Norwegian allies; *Hamlet* begins just after the marriage between Hamlet's mother and his dead father's brother; *Twelfth Night* begins after a storm has shipwrecked Viola and her twin brother. And so on. And this convention is not, of course, restricted to Shakespeare. Modern dramatists generally stick with it. Whether it's as dramatic as the death that has brought three estranged sisters together (*Memory of Water*) or as simple as an eviction requiring that a mother and her daughter find new lodgings (*A Taste of Honey*), often the inciting incident has happened just before the play begins and the characters are trying, in their different ways, to cope with the fallout from that.

Insight

Don't feel that you have to be too dark or too serious in these opening moments of a play. Humour is one of the key things that makes us warm to the characters. We need to be engaged by them if we are going to stay in their company for the next couple of hours. Plays often start with a moment of a release. Even if the event that has brought the characters together is a funeral there is often laughter.

Exercise 85

Choose one of the following scenarios:

A *It is the sixteenth birthday of one of your characters. To celebrate, they bought a lottery scratchcard and have won a large sum of money. On the way home they meet someone else.*

B *One of your characters knew one of the others a long time ago. They meet by chance on a bus.*

C *An elderly person is having trouble coping on their own and someone they know has decided it is time for them to move into sheltered accommodation.*

D *Someone has been offered a new job which means moving away. The character breaks the news to someone close to them.*

You can use characters you came up with earlier or invent new ones. Write 50 words or so about how the conversation might go. What might the characters want to get out of the conversation?

In order to do this exercise well it is very important to think about status and conflict.

Status

Everyone suffers from some kind of status anxiety at least some of the time. Some people suffer from it nearly all of the time. Where do I fit into the world? Are my friends doing better than me? Where am I in the pecking order?

> **Insight**
>
> Status anxiety is a powerful motivating force. It pushes people to achieve great things but also causes huge frustration when we feel blocked or thwarted. It will be important for you as a playwright to know what each of your character's status is. Not just in the sense of whether they have an important job or not, but how they are seen by others and how they feel about themselves.

One of the mistakes King Lear makes is to think that his status will survive his giving over some of his royal powers to his daughters. Your characters will want to maintain or improve their status in the face of the pressures and temptations you give them. It is possible, of course, to have an apparently low-status role but to actually be high status in a particular situation. We all know firms where the cleaners or receptionists seem to have higher status than the bosses; shops where customers about to spend a great deal of money on designer clothes seem to have lower status than the teenage shop assistant serving them; and we all know households where the smallest child seems to rule the roost.

Conflict

This is at the heart of all drama. It doesn't mean violence, fights and arguments (though it might mean all of these) but it does mean that characters must clash. Of course the differing status of your characters may mean that they are not all equally free to express how they feel. A frustrated low-level employee may have to use subtle means to get across their true feelings towards a bullying boss. A shy daughter may have her own methods of conducting a rebellion against what she sees as the harsh rule of a mother.

Insight

Of course, the responses of your characters may not be verbal. Plays are about action, not words.

Exercise 86

1   *Script a short scene between the two characters you used in the last exercise, making sure that first you have given each one a status level out of ten (ten being high and one very low). As you write your script remember that we rarely discuss the perceived status of one another. In conversation we try and maintain the fiction that everybody is equal, though we all usually know that there are certain people whose feathers we try not to ruffle because of their power over us, or because of their worries and insecurities about status.*

2   *Now repeat the exercise but reversing the status levels.*

It is interesting how your characters' efforts to get what they want from a meeting or a conversation are limited by their status. It is interesting too how having a secret can raise or lower a character's status or make them more vulnerable to changes in their status as the scene progresses.

Now rewrite the scene but this time the characters' status must swap over gradually. Your nine must become your one and vice versa. Without being too clumsy or too obvious you need to develop this meeting so that the top dog loses power to the underdog. Aim to do this over two pages of script.

Remember

New writers for the stage often worry too much about the layout of the script. A good producer, director or actor will see quality however it is presented. But that is no reason to make it harder for them than it has to be.

Briefly, you need to set out your script like this:

- ▶ *First page – top right, header with draft number, name of play and author.*
- ▶ *Second page – cast list.*
- ▶ *Third page – Act One, centred.*
- ▶ *Fourth page – Scene One, underlined.*
- ▶ *Only use brackets for stage directions and keep the directions in capitals or italics.*
- ▶ *Have your characters' names in bold on the left and your dialogue clearly separated.*

There are software programs such as Final Draft that will do all this for you and if you are wanting to go on and write more plays, or write for radio or television, then it is probably worth considering investing in one of these.

Tension

Audiences want to care for the characters and they want to worry about them. Your characters should be under some kind of threat or face some kind of choice. How they deal with that threat, or the consequences of their choices, is what provides the tension. They also have to respond to the actions and choices of others. There may be shifting alliances and power-plays between the characters. Remember that changes in characters happen gradually and the fact that you only have an hour or so to make big changes happen means you have to use even more subtlety so that audiences don't think the change is rushed or forced. You have to give proper amounts of time for people to grow and transform. Arguments should heat up slowly and revelations should be drip-fed. Secrets may burst from a character in a sudden rush but there will usually have been clues in their demeanour or body language to the burdens that they have been carrying.

In the previous exercises you dealt with issues of conflict and status between two characters. It will be interesting to see what happens when you add a third issue.

Exercise 88

Look back at exercises 85–87, for two characters, and try and take your scene on with the entrance of a third character. Decide in advance what your third character wants from the scene and what their status is in relation to the others. Now you have a situation where three agendas are competing. Try and aim to add at least another two pages to your script.

Dialogue versus action

As in novels, the speech in plays is not the same as speech in real life, though we often pretend that it is. What you are trying to do is distil the essence of real life. To create believable dialogue which also advances the story you want to tell. The words should sound like they are natural to those characters in that particular situation. And be aware too that your characters will use different words depending on their age, background and education. Some will be more articulate than others. Some will grow more articulate as the scene develops or as their passion about a subject increases. For some, passion will rob them of their usual fluency. It's up to you to make these decisions. And, once again, remember that actions are the key to successful drama, not simply the words.

Insight

Read your lines out loud. This is good practice for all writers but it is especially important for theatre writers. It is only through hearing your characters speak that you can hear the bum notes, the clunky lines. It's even better if you can rope in some competent readers to voice the different parts.

One great modern playwright, Tim Fountain, once said, 'The words in a play are to give the actors something to *do* not something to *say*.' Plays are about characters' actions not their words. In fact, the words of a character might well be to try and disguise their actions. This gives the audience that complicated pleasure known as dramatic irony, by which they know more than the characters do.

If it is to work, your play should be full of action. I don't mean that it should have car chases and sword fights and explosions. It should have the more powerful action of human beings striving to achieve their goals, of trying to balance contradictory impulses.

Not a lot needs to happen in your play, however, for it to be chock full of action and incident. It's just that those events there are, must be full of meaning and significance for the characters in the play.

If a downtrodden wife places a cup a centimetre out of reach of her dictatorial husband when usually she hands it to him directly, this may tell us about the beginnings of a revolt against tyranny. Subtle shifts of power can be detected by an audience in a squabble about who is paying for the coffee.

Each scene of your play is going to see the characters groping towards desires that might be obvious to the audience, but not to the other characters and maybe not even to themselves. Drama is distilled real life, not real life itself, so each word, each line, must be in the script for a purpose. It must move the action along in some way. It must justify itself. Don't use speeches to reveal character. Use action to show character instead. The words characters speak should be there because they *have* to be there. They are things that the characters *have* to say.

Structure

The key to being a good playwright is right there, in the name, *playwright*. First of all, it is *play*. It should be fun. No one wants to go to the theatre to be lectured at. We get enough of that at home, at work, at school. We might hope to learn things from the show but we don't want to notice that we are being taught. And you need to bring a sense of fun and mischief to your drama if you want it to work. Humour is one of the best ways to get an audience caring about your characters right at the start. And we need to care. Even about the characters we learn to despise later. We need to feel involved in them and their struggles, desires and dilemmas.

Insight

Plays are *constructed* as much as they are written. Again the clue is there in the job-title. It's play*wrights* after all, like wheelwrights and shipwrights. Makers of physical entities. If you can think of your play as a physical thing that needs shaping and crafting then you are likely to be more successful than if you just pour your heart out onto the page.

WRITE IN SCENES

This seems obvious. It's a play: of course it will be in scenes. But what I really mean is that each scene should have a rhythm and momentum of its own. As well as staging posts on the way to the final resolution of the piece, they should be complete in themselves with their own tensions, secrets, desires and resolutions. Each scene is like a play in itself, one that also advances the plot and action of the work as a whole.

Insight

Keep your scenes tight in terms of space and time. Audiences often find very short scenes and large gaps in time very off-putting in a theatrical context.

Exercise 89

Look at the scene you have written. Write out an arc for each of the characters. What is the journey that each of them makes? How are they going to be changed by the events that take place? Write the main story making sure that all the characters suffer some ups and downs as the play progresses. Now try and break that story into five further scenes, five little episodes that will reveal a bit more of the various stories of your three characters as they intersect with each other. Make notes about what will happen in each scene. Remember, each scene should be like a play in itself with its own beginning, middle and end.

A SINGULAR SETTING

A lot of plays which have continued pleasing audiences over many years have taken place in one unchanging setting. Often this can be one room. At the time of writing I have had two plays produced and the first of these took place entirely in the rehearsal room of a small-time rock band and the other in a girl's bedroom.

The multiple locations and sudden shifts between them that work in film can be jarring for a theatre audience and hard to pull off on stage. As you get more experienced you will find ways of getting around this problem; for now, however, you will find it easier to restrict your characters' movements. Many great plays have been set in one room. Think of Arthur Miller and *The Crucible* where the action takes place largely in the courthouse, or Oscar Wilde where it is mostly in drawing rooms over tea, or Samuel Beckett where characters hardly move from one spot.

It was the Ancient Greeks who first came up with the rules that have for thousands of years governed the way that theatre works. Obviously these have been meddled with and experimented with many times over the centuries but still audiences respond best to a play that respects what Aristotle called the unities of Time, Place and Action. People still most like a play that begins at the beginning and moves in a linear fashion to a conclusion.

Lastly, theatre seems to be the place where our common humanity can be best played out. It is a more intimate, more shared experience than any other art form. Stories, novels and poems are often private communions between writer and reader, while films are often huge spectacles removed from our everyday experience by the sheer size of the screen as well as by the Hollywood subject matter. Television often has the opposite effect. We watch actors and stories shrunk to a less than human size and we watch them in our private or family spaces. It is only really stage drama that gives us a sense of ourselves. Crammed together in the dark watching living, breathing people a few feet away grappling with the pain of living... What could be more life-affirming than that? Even if it has cost us a fortune in babysitters and overpriced Merlot?

Exercise 90

Write a short play for your three characters. Aim for between 10 and 15 minutes, (or about 10 pages). Each character should be changed by the end and the status that they began with altered too.

How to market your play

Theatres often have a Literary Manager whose job it is to read new scripts with a view to possible performance. The more conscientious or progressive theatres will ensure that they give detailed feedback on scripts, though you may have to wait a while as they get dozens of scripts every single week.

In addition, many theatres have a playwrights' group where you can meet other writers and discuss your work. These theatres may also run a programme where new writers can get the opportunity to have their work read or workshopped, and these can be very useful places to start. The theatres that have these programmes will very often have one-act play festivals to which you can submit work. You should see if there is a theatre locally that has a scheme like this. If nothing else it is very often a chance to meet theatre professionals and find out what is currently exciting them.

Other theatres will run competitions to which new writers can submit work and often theatres will follow up promising writers even if they don't use the particular play that was submitted.

Many regions of the UK and most districts of the USA have thriving playwright networks which offer mutual support to emerging writers. Touring companies are also often on the lookout for exciting new work. Try and find out about as many of these as you can – see their shows. Since the decline of the old Rep theatres (many of which defy the odds and cling on), the touring theatre companies have become the place where a lot of important theatre professionals learn their craft. This includes actors, directors and producers as well as writers. Many of these companies are small outfits formed by actors just out of drama school, attempting to generate their own work so as not to be reliant simply on the vagaries of the job market. A lot of these companies will be interested in reading scripts that the bigger theatres just won't want to take a chance on.

Another thing worth doing is to try and get a director who will champion your work. It is often easier to get a director on board than a theatre – there are a lot more of them for a start and they are also looking for work that excites them.

Another route to try is drama schools which are often looking for scripts that will challenge their students, or amateur companies which, at the very least might, might be willing to give your play a rehearsed reading.

Insight

If you are going to have actors speak your words you should at least experience how they feel. Join a theatre group and get used to the difficulties of playing a part. You needn't be an actor, but become involved somehow. You can stage manage, build sets or sell tickets, but you should try and be around plays as they are put together. You should try to develop a feel for the mechanics of it.

Adaptation

Adapting a novel or, increasingly, a film for the stage can be a useful way into writing for the theatre. Audiences – and producers! – often like to minimize the risks involved in a night at the theatre by ensuring that they already know the story. Or at least that the story is one which has already stood the test of time. It means that you don't have to worry so much about creating character or plot. That's already done for you, though deciding what to cut while retaining the essential vitality of the original is a special surgical skill of its own.

A good way of beginning an adaptation without getting bogged down in the minutiae of a novel's plots and subplots is to read the original (or watch the film) carefully twice and then put it aside and write out a three-page synopsis. What you have kept in is probably the heart of the story. Or at least, those aspects of the story that engage you most directly.

Insight

If you choose to adapt a well-loved piece expect to take some flak from its devotees. It might be more interesting for you as a writer to try to find a work that hasn't been done too often. Something unusual. A forgotten or neglected classic.

Professional tip from Willy Russell

When writing a play the most important thing is to do it – not talk about doing it, intend to do it, mean to do it, plan to do it or dream of doing it. Do it. The world is full of those who talk about doing it, dream, mean, intend, plan to do it – when they find the right time or the right place or the right computer, the right pen, the right paper, the right frame of mind. The writer knows that there is no right this or right that and to write a play (or indeed anything else) you have to DO IT. Good luck.

Willy Russell is the author of many successful stage plays including *Blood Brothers*, *Educating Rita* and *Shirley Valentine* (Heinemann).

10 THINGS TO REMEMBER

1 *Do your homework. See new writing at your local theatre.*

2 *Join a theatre group.*

3 *Make your characters real, flawed human beings.*

4 *Write for small casts.*

5 *Use humour. Make your audience laugh if you can. The earlier in the play the better.*

6 *Know the status of your characters.*

7 *Make sure there is conflict between your characters.*

8 *Allow arguments between characters time to heat up.*

9 *Plays are about characters in action. They are not about not speeches.*

10 *Dialogue exists to give characters something to do, rather than something to say.*

17

Writing radio plays

In this chapter you will learn:
- *the importance of thinking visually*
- *the advantages of a narrator*
- *how to use sound*
- *where to send your radio play.*

> *Radio is the theatre of the mind; television is the theatre of the mindless.*
>
> Steve Allen

The BBC

One of the things that is great about the UK is the BBC. It might not feel like it sometimes as we are bullied into going digital whether we want to or not, and when we find that, despite an ever-increasing licence fee, there seems to be nothing on television but talent contests, quizzes and reality shows. Nevertheless, a state-funded (but not state-controlled) television and radio service dedicated to entertaining and informing without necessarily worrying about commercial interests or ratings, is a rare privilege and the envy of the entire developed world. And one of the glories of the BBC is the continuing interest in radio drama.

There is nowhere else in the world where as much effort is put into radio plays. BBC radio creates high-quality drama featuring some of the world's best-known actors and brightest writing stars every single day. The production values on BBC radio drama are incredibly high and the range of styles and subjects is immense. Of course not all the dramas broadcast on BBC Radio 3 and 4 are produced in-house. There are many smaller production companies that produce work commissioned by the BBC. And there are other networks that produce radio drama, though not in the same quantity as the Beeb.

Writers in the USA and other countries do not have the same access to radio plays (though NPR in the States still produces some). Writers from other countries are, however, not barred from writing for the UK market. And, with the advent of the internet, the output of the BBC is available to anyone who cares to listen. A little bit of time and trouble and the American, Australian or, indeed, Siberian writer, can listen to the BBC's high-quality radio drama and get a feel for this exciting medium.

Liberation

Writing radio drama has been the springboard for many great writers, while those who have made their name in other areas, such as film or theatre or poetry, still like to return to writing for radio because of some of the special benefits it offers.

Most theatre or even film directors would blanch at the idea of a story that takes place in outer space, features talking dolphins and travels through many centuries in time. Yet in radio all of this is possible. It is even, in the case of *The Hitchhiker's Guide To The Galaxy* (which began life as a series on BBC Radio 4), possible within the same piece of work. By using sound to unlock the listener's imagination there is no setting that need be ruled out on grounds of cost or practicality. If your play features two pit ponies conducting a love affair down a mineshaft in the early years of the seventeenth century then this is entirely feasible.

A writer for radio has the freedom to write about any subject, any idea and set their story in any time in history including the distant future. You can write about real figures, without worrying about getting an actor who looks like the historical character. You can also write in several lengths. There are slots for 30-minute, 45-minute, 60-minute and 90-minute plays. And then there are dramas in several parts.

> **Insight**
> A writer for radio is released from a lot of the usual constraints that inhibit the stage dramatist. Radio can be the most liberating medium of them all.

This doesn't mean that it is an easy medium. All the other rules of drama – engaging characters, conflict, narrative drive, tension, vivid believable dialogue, an awareness of status – still apply. In fact your words must be even better because, despite all the other things that a skilled radio producer and director can bring to the piece, it is essentially your words that are going to sustain an audience's interest. And there are some major additional obstacles to overcome to produce a worthwhile piece of radio writing.

The vision thing

The radio dramatist is utilizing the most powerful tool a writer can have: the imagination of the audience. We've discussed elsewhere that audiences like to work, they like to become actively engaged with the action no matter what medium the story is told in. In radio the writer's chief skill lies in helping the audience to picture the setting, characters and events. This means that the language of the play can be heightened. Whereas in stage drama a lot can be gauged through action and gesture, on radio the language has to carry a lot more of the weight. This is why it can be such a great medium for poets who are already used to writing in images. You have to create a vivid image in the listener's mind from sound alone and though there is a lot that can be done with sound effects, still the writer is going to have to ensure that there is enough visual detail in the words for the listener's imagination to feed on.

Insight

This *doesn't* mean that the writer needs to use lots of adjectives. *Don't* have your characters mention the 'vast blue sky' or similar clichés, but you should at least think about colour and description in your dialogue.

Exercise 91

Look out of the window nearest to your writing desk. Take a mental photograph. Now move away from the scene – turn your back if you have to – and write a detailed description in such a way that a reader or a listener could picture it exactly. Aim for 100 words. After you have done this, look again. What have you missed out?

Exercise 92

Now, imagine some kind of crime has taken place outside your window. It can be minor or serious. Then, imagine that a patient, experienced policeman is trying to coax a description of the offence from a witness. This simple exercise gives you an inciting incident, two strong characters in the policeman and the witness, some tension as the witness describes the event and some human engagement because we can all sympathize with the victims of crime and empathize with the situation of both the witness and the copper. But it also tests your power to create pictures inside a listener's head.

Direct address

One of the chief pleasures of writing for radio is that you can use direct address. This simply means a character telling a story directly to the audience. It can be a very powerful tool on the stage too, but writers (and audiences!) are nervous of it as it seems to disturb the illusion in which we are unseen, unnoticed spectators as events unfold on stage. Theatre folk often talk about the 'fourth wall' meaning the imaginary, invisible barrier that divides the audience from the actors (the other three walls being those at the side and behind the stage). The idea that someone can talk through this wall directly to the audience can still seem disturbing and dangerously experimental to some people.

In radio, by contrast, it is almost essential. In radio a character speaking thoughts out loud in a stream of consciousness is a completely valid, universally accepted device. It is because of this that radio is the natural place for those who love the idea of writing monologues.

Insight

Characters talking from the heart about their innermost feelings and key memories, and doing it directly into the head of the listener, is one of the most powerful and intimate exchanges that writers can have with their audience.

Exercise 93

Write a short monologue about a key memory from your past. Perhaps a secret or something that you have only told a very few people. Try and choose something that you think has shaped the person that you have become now. Don't worry about how personal it is or how upsetting. In any case no one but you has to read it. You can always destroy your writing as soon as you have completed this exercise. I bet you don't though.

Remember Hemingway's advice to a writer, 'Write hard about what hurts.' In the end what was painful or hurtful to us becomes material that we can process for the entertainment and enlightenment of others. One of the joys of being a writer is that we can use the hurt of the past to bring complicated but lasting pleasure into the present.

Insight

Using a narrator in radio drama is very useful as a device to move the listener between scenes. This is common in radio drama where a narrator also becomes a way of turning the stage directions into part of the action. The narrator is also useful for describing the passage of time.

Exercise 94

1 *Write two short scenes. The first is between a young boy and his mother. The boy is five years old and it is his first day of school. He is seeking to reassure his anxious mother that he will be all right.*

2 *The second scene takes place 13 years later. The boy is now 18 years old and about to leave home to go to university. The conversation mirrors the first one, though of course it will have some key differences as the boy is now grown up.*

3 *Now write a third scene where either the mother or the son describes in a few sentences what has happened to the two of them in the years between the two scenes. You can make this linking scene more powerful by addressing it to the person who isn't narrating. In other words, the mother will address the son as 'you' or vice versa.*

Putting the listener in the position of a person being talked to is also more effective on radio than in the theatre. In the theatre we are always slightly conscious of all the other people around us, so when a character addresses us as 'you' the intimacy is never entirely convincing. On radio, because we are usually listening on our own, it is easier to be drawn into the illusion of identifying with the person being talked to.

Including sound

It seems obvious but as a radio writer you will need to be thinking constantly about sound in the same way that a stage writer must always be thinking about action. You should be meticulous in making sure that your scripts are full of sounds that tell the reader where they are and what is happening.

Insight
You'll be amazed at how sound, deployed well, will save you – and, more importantly, the listener – from the tedium of your characters describing absolutely everything.

Exercise 95

1 *Imagine the road outside your house early on a typical morning. Describe it solely in terms of the sounds you hear. Are there children singing? Mothers shouting? Sirens? Birds singing? Traffic? How do the sounds build up?*
2 *Now repeat the exercise for a typical night.*
3 *Lastly write the sounds of a crime taking place in the street outside. You might hear voices but there might well be a lot else that's going on as well. Try to make your scene as dramatic as possible.*

MUSIC

Music is evocative in all forms of drama, but for radio writers it is an essential way to develop moods. Songs can place your audience immediately in a particular place and time. Music can act as an extremely effective form of shorthand, a great way to set a scene without the need for dialogue explaining where the characters are. It was Noël Coward who coined the line about 'the potency of cheap music' (and he should know), and it is true that popular music can add a great deal of resonance to a piece.

Fashions in music tend to come in waves. Rock and roll burst onto the cultural scene in the middle of the 1950s. The Beatles changed everything again in the early 1960s. Glam, progressive rock, heavy metal, disco and punk all staked their claims in the 1970s, while the 1980s saw the dominance of synthesizer bands and the New Romantics as well as the birth of hip-hop and rap.

From 'Rock Around The Clock' up to the recent hits by the Kaiser Chiefs, pop music has sound-tracked the lives of generations of teenagers. It might be that the very ubiquity of popular music now has diluted its impact, but for the radio writer songs can still help set the tone, and even help tell the story of a piece. They don't do this in the obvious way that the songs in a musical do, but the songs of a period can provide a sly subplot of their own that gives support or contrast to the main action.

Exercise 96

Choose three or four key moments in your life that you think you might like to write about one day. Now write down the songs that were important at these times. They can be those that had special significance for you personally (perhaps they were songs you had played at your wedding? Or at a family funeral?) or they can simply be what was in the charts or on the radio at the time.

THE SOUND OF SILENCE

In a stage drama, silence can be very powerful. It gives the audience a chance to focus on the body language of the actors.

Their gestures, movements, facial expressions, the way that they handle the props, all of these can be very revealing. Some of the most powerful scenes ever performed achieved their impact through the agonizing gaps between the words. Beckett and Pinter are the acknowledged masters of the art of silence but there are others too.

It is also possible to use silence well on radio. However, if the pause goes on for more than a couple of seconds your listeners may assume that there has been a power cut and will start fiddling with the dials. This is the last thing you want. Using silence in radio drama is like using a rare and precious spice in cooking – the finest saffron say – you want to be very careful not to waste it.

Where to send your radio script

The BBC has a number of initiatives designed to help new writers and writers wanting to work on radio drama in particular. Perhaps the best place to start is the Writers' Room: www.bbc.co.uk/writersroom.

The BBC is also involved in the Alfred Bradley Award which is a competition run with the express purpose of finding new writers for radio. Each shortlisted entrant receives the chance to develop work for radio while the winner also gets £5,000 and their work broadcast. The competition is a great way to get your work noticed and gives you something to aim for. It is also judged by writers of a high calibre so that you know your efforts are being read by the best of your peers.

Insight

You should also be considering sending your work to producers whom you admire. If you are serious about writing for radio you will be listening to a lot of plays and you will always find the name of the producer listed in the end credits, which will also tell you which studio the play was recorded in.

Remember

Script layout should be as follows:

Macbeth (this title will go on each page)

Ambience: A wild storm in a deserted place. Wind. Rain etc. etc.

1 First Witch   When shall we three meet again
                 In thunder, lightning or in rain
2 Second Witch When the hurly-burly's done

SOUND EFFECT THUNDER

▶ *Remember to put text on one side of the page only and
   don't let a speech run over to the next page.*
▶ *Note that all speeches rather than individual lines are
   numbered.*
▶ *If you want an actor to give emphasis to a particular
   word or phrase then simply underline it.*
▶ *Keep your stage directions to a minimum.*

OTHER RADIO OUTLETS

Up to now we have focused largely on the BBC who, through
Radio 3 and 4 and the World Service, produce the majority of
radio drama in the UK. But there are other stations, particularly
those that use the internet as a way of broadcasting material. As
audiences for niche programming and community-based stations
grow then we may find that these become increasingly important
outlets for drama.

SOME LEADING RADIO WRITERS

The work of those specializing in writing radio drama does not
attract the attention given to writers in other media and it can be
hard to find examples of their work. But you should try and track

down plays by Lee Hall, Marcy Khan, Mike Walker, Mark Illis, Amanda Dalton and Nell Leyshon, all of whom have produced marvellous work for radio.

Professional tip from Mark Illis

Over-formal, over-grammatical, on-the-nose dialogue will drain the life out of your writing. Make sure there's a subtext; remember how people tend not to answer questions directly – or at all; start the scene late and get out early. And dialogue is probably the easiest thing to over-write, because it acquires its own momentum, so revise ruthlessly.

Mark Illis has written numerous radio plays that have been broadcast on BBC Radio 4. He also writes for film and television.

5 THINGS TO REMEMBER

1 *Radio gives opportunities to a lot of writers.*

2 *Writers for radio have the freedom to range across the whole of time and space.*

3 *Make sure your scripts are full of sound (as well as fury...).*

4 *Use music to help tell your story.*

5 *Avoid on-the-nose, over-formal dialogue.*

18

Screenwriting

In this chapter you will learn:
- *the basic television formats*
- *the differences between film and television*
- *how to begin writing collaboratively*
- *about opportunities for new screenwriters.*

> *The theatre is like a faithful wife. The film is the great adventure – the costly exacting mistress.*
>
> Ingmar Bergman

> *Television is the first truly democratic culture – the first culture available to everybody and entirely governed by what the people want. The most terrifying thing is what the people do want.*
>
> Clive Barnes

Why write for television?

The main attraction of writing for television is the potential for having your work seen by millions. It is also a medium that is voracious in its demand for stories. There are now hundreds of television channels that need to fill thousands of hours. Granted, a lot of those hours are taken up with talk shows, sport, adverts, old films, cartoons, reality shows, quizzes and reruns of past television shows – but there is still a large market hungry for fresh, innovative material.

Basic formats of television drama

THE CLOSED SERIAL

This is a story that comes to an end over several parts. The lengths of these dramas can vary. It is common to see two-part dramas where each part is an hour or two hours long. (These are often screened over two nights in the UK.) A story can also be told over six parts or more – in the form of a weekly serial. The benefit for writers of these longer serials is that they have time to develop character and drama in a more thorough way than would be possible in a programme shown over just a couple of nights. They have some of the novelist's luxury when it comes to taking time to move the story on.

The hope is that a weekly serial becomes a family event where everyone sits down together at the same time each week to watch *Prime Suspect* or an Andrew Davies adaptation of a classic novel.

Increasingly, technology means that these serials are not necessarily viewed at the same time each week but that people are watching at times which suit them. Tivo, Sky Plus and the various 'on demand' formats have put viewers very much more in charge of their television programming than ever before. Viewers can, in effect, create their own viewing schedules which can make life difficult for television executives trying to tie an audience to a television 'appointment'. Also, viewers often now wait for the box set of a popular series to appear on DVD so that they can have the benefit of the reviews and the word of mouth about a programme before committing the time to watching it.

Social changes too have meant a corresponding change in television-watching habits. Most families have several televisions, so the chances of the whole family gathering together to watch the same show at the same time is increasingly unlikely. Nevertheless this remains the holy grail of much television programming.

Insight

A crossover show that appeals to parents, to young professionals and to at least older children is a show that is going to be talked about and attract advertisers.

THE ONE-HOUR DRAMA SERIES

This is a number of self-contained episodes. The plot will have its own three-act structure but the characters will be the same week to week and will contain storylines that the audience are familiar with. Our enjoyment of the story will be enriched by our knowledge of the protagonists and the struggles they have outside of the main plotline. One-hour drama series that work well are shows like *Without A Trace*.

THE SOAP

The soap is usually a half-hour open series that can be on several nights a week, featuring a cast of much-loved characters based around one central location such as Albert Square for *EastEnders* or Southfork ranch in *Dallas*. These can run for years and the storylines will reflect the dramas of ordinary life. They are intended to be realistic: a distillation of real life. Each soap will have started life with a 'Bible' that contains all the details of the characters and the locations.

Soaps are enormously popular but comparatively cheap to shoot and so can be the most effective kind of television drama. Soap operas and other long-term series use storyliners to develop the plots, while writers are responsible for the dialogue and action of each individual episode. A typical soap opera might have up to 30 writers and half a dozen storyliners working on its production.

THE HALF-HOUR SITCOM

Television is always on the lookout for new comedy writing talent. It is also the area where there is most likely to be a level playing field. When it comes to writing comedy it either makes the audience laugh, in which case it is a success, or it doesn't, in which case it's a failure.

Insight

For comedy it doesn't matter who you know or if you've got a track record. If your script makes executives laugh then you are in with a shout of getting television to take a chance on you.

Situation comedies of the classic kind like *Friends* and *I Love Lucy* in the USA or, in the UK, *Steptoe and Son, Are You Being Served?* and *The Likely Lads* – that have a few strong comic characters in one location – have rather fallen from favour in recent years and most comedies now seem to include a drama or soap opera element. The classic sitcom often seemed to be about class struggle. In *Steptoe and Son* Harold Steptoe is forever trying to escape the role of rag-and-bone man and make something of himself, only to find his father continually bringing him down. In *Whatever Happened To The Likely Lads?* Bob Ferris wants to leave behind the macho working-class culture he grew up with for a more bourgeois life with his posh new wife, but his childhood friend, the feckless Terry Collier, does everything he can to remind Bob of where he really belongs. In the more modern sitcoms focus has switched to struggles between the sexes rather than struggles over class identity. For example, *Men Behaving Badly*, where the two male protagonists resist growing up and settling down by any means necessary, while at the same time appeasing their long-suffering girlfriends.

In so far as it is possible to spot contemporary trends, they seem to be about the battle of eccentric characters to maintain themselves within the confines of a conformist world. Think of *Green Wing* or *Black Books*. This theme can also be detected in spoofs like *Life on Mars* where a modern, politically correct cop finds himself catapulted back in time to a rougher, more forthright world.

In the USA, comedies like *Seinfeld* or *The Larry Sanders Show* differ in that they are built around characters who have worldly success, though they also have unlikeable and selfish traits. It is this self-obsession, a basic inability to empathize, that gets the characters into scrapes. Again in a comedy like *The Office* it is a character's self-delusion that provides the humour. He sees himself as a King of Comedy, the wit of his workplace, universally loved and admired, whereas in truth David Brent is unable to connect at an ordinary, functional level.

In general, popular American comedies tend to be more life affirming and more obviously heartwarming. In *Seinfeld* the characters might lead gleefully empty lives (it is, after all, famously a 'show about nothing') but at least they are a supportive, close-knit unit. This is taken to a further extreme in *Friends*, where the whole premise is of a group ethos, where individual quirks are sublimated to a team ideal. The message of a sitcom like *Friends* is that we are greater together than we are alone. That whatever conflicts we have, they can be resolved by the intervention and love of our closest buddies.

This is also the message from influential comedies like *Cheers*, its spin-off *Frasier* and from shows like *Roseanne*. Individuals might fight, but in the end family or group loyalty will enable problems to be resolved. Even a character as ostensibly selfish as Larry David in *Curb Your Enthusiasm* is redeemed by his relationship with his long-suffering wife and with his old friends.

Insight

Remember, the boundaries between all these formats can seem blurred these days. Take *Shameless*, for example, or *Desperate Housewives*. Are these comedies? One-hour drama series? Soaps? All three? It's hard to decide.

Where to start

If you feel that you can create strong characters, fast-moving plots and can write realistic witty dialogue and, best of all, think visually, then it might be that television is the medium for you. And the best way to start is to write your own script. Don't write a version of one of the series or serials that are already out there. Try something completely new. Even if your dream is to write for *Coronation Street* or *Scrubs* eventually, don't start by writing a script for that show. Try something original. You'll have much more chance of impressing producers if you can come up with something where you have had to think of all the characters and stories yourself.

STRUCTURE

Whatever kind of television you want to write you will need to conform to the structural rules of that format. The first thing to bear in mind is length. A half-hour programme is actually 23 minutes. Similarly an hour is 55 minutes. And these are inflexible rules. It's not like the theatre where a piece can be roughly 90 minutes long. Television doesn't recognize rough lengths. Work on each page of your script being roughly 40 seconds of airtime.

You should also adhere to the three-act structure. Beginning, middle and end, with characters in jeopardy right from the get-go. This is true even if you are writing the first episode of what you hope will become a long-running show.

The outline

The first thing you need is an idea. A one-sentence concept which excites your imagination. The first television series I attempted began as a simple 'What if…'. What if you could meet your own 18-year-old self? Simple. But exciting. I put it to my writing partner (television writing is often done collaboratively, and I'll say more about this later in the chapter) and he was sufficiently enthused to suggest we start putting together an outline immediately.

An outline is a short synopsis explaining the key characters and setting out the general plot. It needs to be written in as engaging a manner as possible. It should also be no more than two pages of double-spaced A4. The idea behind the outline is partly to give yourself a map through to the finished script, but also to intrigue potential producers enough so that they want to see the script. When you are an established television writer it might be that this outline is all you need to get producers excited and they will commission a script (one which they will pay for) on the strength of this alone. Before you reach those heights it will always be best to have an actual script to show.

Here is an example of the first paragraph of an outline for a new television show.

Teenage Kicks by M. I. and Stephen May

> The 18-year-old son you never knew you had shows up out of the blue. And he's embarrassing. He follows you around, heckling you all the time, because he thinks you've made too many compromises and wrong turnings. Why are you coming up with designs for sweet wrappers when you were going to be an artist? They call you Steady Eddie at work. What's that about? And you're getting married? Why?

> Under that sort of pressure, you're bound to start questioning yourself. All right this boy is immature. And naïve. And yes, irritating and self-centred and obsessed by sex. But all the same – are you where you want to be? Have you made a grown-up, realistic accommodation with life, or have you just thrown away your dreams and buckled under?

> But supposing your son does successfully pull the rug out from under you. Supposing you try to live the way he wants you to live. Is that likely to work out for a man who's knocking 40, with a mortgage and a fiancée?

Teenage Kicks suggests you might have something to learn from a younger, more idealistic voice. But it would be dangerous to get too carried away ...

After you have an outline you can begin working on a scene breakdown. Scenes need to be short. Probably far shorter than you realize. A one-hour television script may have 90 scenes or more. It will rarely have fewer than 70.

Your scene-by-scene breakdown may not contain absolutely every scene that goes into your eventual script but it is important that you have a step-by-step route plan to keep you focused on the story. Your characters will reveal themselves through their actions far more than through their dialogue. Remember that in television it is even more important that you show not tell. Television is a visual, technical medium where dialogue is always suppressed to make way for action. This is as true for comedy as it is for any other format, by the way.

Here is an example of the scene breakdown of the show which the outline came from:

7. INT. OFFICE/SARAH'S HOUSE

We see BARRY in action in the office. He's in a bad mood. He thought Eddie would be in early today of all days. And why couldn't he get him on his mobile? A naked EDDIE claims he's on the bus, but BARRY is uninterested in EDDIE'S excuses. He's busy being vile to his staff KERRY, PAUL and JANICE. The call ends. The moment really has gone now. SARAH and EDDIE briefly reflect on what the promotion might mean. A new bathroom for one thing. EDDIE affects not to be too bothered. As long as that pushy young thing KERRY doesn't get it. 'You really don't like her do you?' SARAH is sympathetic and then reminds him that they have a dirty weekend away. Not too long to wait.

8. INT. OFFICE

BARRY sends home a passing work experience kid for 'looking at him funny'. Oh yes, he's on form today.

9. SARAH'S HOUSE

A near-naked EDDIE watches from the window as ROB
collects SARAH for her lift to school. He's irritated to see
ROB give SARAH a social kiss on the cheek. EDDIE checks
the time. Shit.

10. EXT. THE STREETS

EDDIE is running again. For the bus this time. We see the
kid from scene 1 following him. He's not going to make the
bus. As he gives up, the black kid runs past him and makes the
bus. EDDIE puts another spurt on but the doors close
in his face.

11. INT. THE OFFICE

BARRY hires YOUNG EDDIE to replace the fired intern.
YOUNG EDDIE wasn't really seeking employment but
BARRY is hard to refuse. KERRY gives BARRY some lip.
He doesn't like that.

Only when you have a very clear and detailed sense of your plot
should you start on your script.

Exercise 97

1   *Take a favourite short story and rewrite it as an outline
    for a television drama series.*
2   *Now break it down into scenes.*

Layout

Remember

Use Final Draft (www.finaldraft.com), or similar software, to make setting out your script as easy as possible and the finished product look professional. These are the basic rules:

- ▶ **Font:** *Courier New 12.*
- ▶ **Spacing:** *single line spacing for action, character name and dialogue. Insert a double space between scene headings and action, and between scenes.*
- ▶ **Page numbering:** *top right.*
- ▶ **Scene heading (aka the slug line):** *this is always in upper case, which makes it easy for production to count the number of times you use a particular location.*
- ▶ **INT.** *= interior or indoors: this is for any scene where characters are inside, whether it is a castle or a car.*
- ▶ **EXT.** *= exterior or outdoors: any scene where the characters are outdoors.*
- ▶ **Action:** *this is the 'business', i.e. what actually takes place in a scene. Keep it visual and concise. Your style describing scenes is an important part of the script – don't neglect it. Don't describe the characters' feelings or state of mind.*
- ▶ **Characters' names:** *capitalize so that those involved in production can see when a new character enters the action.*
- ▶ **Dialogue:** *indent with the character's name in capitals over the dialogue.*
- ▶ **Sounds:** *significant sounds are capitalized, e.g. SIRENS WAIL.*
- ▶ **Parentheses:** *use very occasionally to tell the producer or actor how a line is delivered. Don't use for action.*

Here is an example of a television script layout.

INT. DESIGN REPUBLIC 09:36 THURS

EDDIE COMES INTO THE OFFICE. AS THEY CLOCK
HIM, EVERYONE BREAKS UP FROM WHERE THEY ARE
AND GETS ON WITH THEIR WORK.

PAUL

What time do you call this?

EDDIE (SV)

Have I got the job? Have you heard?

BARRY AND A SLIGHTLY TENSE KERRY HAVE
APPROACHED. KERRY IS 26, TALENTED, SPARKY AND
AMBITIOUS, AND CLEARLY DOESN'T FIT IN
AT DESIGN REPUBLIC.

BARRY

I call it nine thirty six, which makes you six minutes late.

EDDIE

Sorry, I know, but it's out of character, you have to admit ...
Hi, Kerry.

KERRY

Eddie.

EDDIE

All right?

KERRY

Fine.

BARRY

That's what I love about office life, all the witty banter.

Note: SV = *sotto voce*. Latin for under his breath.

A calling card script

You need a script if you are going to have a career in writing for television. It's the only way anyone will tell if you are any good. It should be as good and as polished a script as you can make it. The chances are that it will never be made but it should show you at your best. It is obviously in your best interests to show producers that you are not only a gifted writer but that you are professional and painstaking. There are lots of agents that deal with television scriptwriters and the advice contained in Chapter 19, 'Agents and publishers', will help you with those. Also look for the names of producers on the end credits of programmes you admire. If you think that your work is in a similar area then these will be names to send you spec script to ('spec' is simply short for speculative and means a script that no one has commissioned). It should, by now, go without saying that you should read plenty of examples of scripts before writing your own. And of course watch as many quality examples of your chosen formats as you can. Become an expert in your chosen medium.

WHERE TO SEND YOUR CALLING CARD SCRIPT

The *Writers' and Artists' Yearbook* contains a comprehensive list of all the main production companies, together with information about the kind of projects they are involved in. Another route into television is the BBC Writers' Room, www.bbc.co.uk/writersroom.

Writing collaboratively

More than any other medium television writing is one where collaboration is common, indeed the norm in some genres. Many new shows have a lead writer, known as a 'show-runner', who leads a committee writing process where ideas are batted about and lines are argued over until it is quite unclear who was the final writer on any one episode. This has been common practice in American television writing for years but is quite new to the UK which has for a long time held out for the primacy of the single writer.

Many writers enjoy the challenge of working collaboratively, though it demands flexibility and tolerance from those involved in it. But if you work in television or film you will be working collaboratively with producers, directors, actors, commissioning executives, story editors and script editors in any case. It is therefore a relatively straightforward step to working with another writer.

Insight

If it is working well, a collaboration more than doubles the qualities that each writer brings to the mix. Your good idea provokes another good idea from your partner which provokes a better idea from you and so on. The competitive energy of this kind of piggyback thinking means that you can move forward with a story faster than either of you could on your own. Your partner might spot weak lines and implausible events before you can, while you might have a much better idea for how to resolve Act Three than they do.

I would never attempt to write a novel or a story with another writer, but there is something about the story-driven and visual impulse of television that makes it right for collaborative work. Of course you need to be able to fight for your ideas and sometimes the partnership won't feel like an equal one. If it was your initial idea the final result might be 70:30 yours, there may even be times when whole segments or whole episodes are 90:10. What you hope is that the work will balance out over time.

SONGWRITERS AS EXAMPLE

The best model for collaborative working is probably the songwriting partnership of John Lennon and Paul McCartney of The Beatles. The two of them wrote fairly few 50:50 compositions, but instead brought unfinished work to one another for completion. Sometimes they would bring complete, finished numbers to each other for checking and quality control. These would then be worked up and arranged in the studio with the rest of the band and their producer.

Television is very different from songwriting but the impulse behind a good collaboration should be the same. You should achieve more together than either of you would do separately. Writing together you should add up to more than the sum of your parts. My television writing partner has a measured, thoughtful way of working that complements my more spontaneous approach and often acts as a brake on my wilder instincts. I do write for television on my own, but I enjoy the sessions with my partner more. Writing in tandem with someone else is not for everyone – it can be frustrating to have to justify your ideas, though in television you will always have to do that sooner or later and best perhaps to do it at an early stage with a friend rather than with a coldly professional commissioning executive. It's definitely worth experimenting with.

Insight

A lot of television is written in teams (this is especially true in the USA). Programmes have a 'show-runner', a lead writer who is responsible for the shape of the programme who will work with a team who will all chip in ideas and stories, even for those episodes that others will write.

Exercise 98

Meet for one afternoon with another writer whose work you admire. They can be from a writers' group or someone you know socially with an interest in writing. Each of you must bring three ideas for stories to the meeting. Agree in advance that this collaboration is a one-off. Decide which of the ideas is best and try and work up a one-page outline. You'll know from this short experiment whether further collaboration is for you, or whether you are a lone wolf.

Writing for film

Television treats writers rather better than the film industry. With film the first question to be asked of any project is 'Who's the star?', whereas with television they do at least ask 'Who are the writers?'.

The most obvious difference between film and television is that television shrinks stories to less than life-size and so perhaps makes more noise and melodrama to compensate. Film, on the other hand, blows up characters and stories to many times human scale. This means, paradoxically, that good film writing is about restraint and understatement.

Insight
Television is essentially a domestic, often solitary experience, while film is a communal event.

Films are never serials. They follow a three-act structure during which time we must get to know all the characters well and have an emotional investment in them.

There is, in the UK at least, almost no demand for British film writers. Very few full-length British films are made and those that are often don't make it into cinemas. And those that get as far as the multiplexes are usually written by a handful of highly experienced writers with great track records, such as Peter Morgan (*The Queen*), Tim Firth (*Calendar Girls*) and Richard Curtis (*Four Weddings and a Funeral*) all of whom wrote extensively for television first.

Star talent

I remember attending a lecture by the film producer Nik Powell (*Scandal*, *The Crying Game*, etc.) where he said that his idea of a good script was 'one that the talent likes'. If you can get big name talent attached then you are a lot further forward with your project whether it is for film or television. There's no mystery to how this is done. If you have a film script that you are proud of you can send it to the agent of your star and hope that they love it enough to consider the role. This in turn gives you some leverage with the various power brokers that put together film financing. It helps if it is your agent punting the script towards the star's agent if only because it means that you have some track record within the industry, some clout.

The problem is, of course, that the 'talent' has no more informed idea of what constitutes a good script than anyone else. Indeed their judgement might be clouded by all sorts of random factors such as 'How long am I on screen for?', 'Will the script make me look ridiculous?', 'Who is my love interest?'. These questions might be very important to the star but getting the answers they want doesn't mean that the script is a good one.

You may not ever get the star you dream of when writing a film, but it is worth at least having an actor in mind when writing it. This can provide you with an important focus. If you can't think of an actor that might fit the film, then perhaps your characters aren't as clearly defined as you had thought. Or perhaps your film is out of step with the current marketplace. This is not necessarily a bad thing, but it does mean that perhaps you should look at your characters again.

Those who rail against the star system should consider just how much it costs to make a mainstream feature film. Even for a relatively low-budget British film you can be talking upwards of £20 million. With this kind of money at stake it is no wonder that producers will do all they can to protect their investment and, like it or not, who the lead actors are is top of most people's list when it comes to deciding what movie to see.

The short film

There is a way to become a film writer without having a track record already, and that is to write a short film. There are lots of organizations dedicated to providing writing and directing opportunities for those interested in short films. Audiences are tiny and opportunities to exhibit the films are generally limited to specialist festivals but nevertheless it is something that the novice film writer should consider.

Most short films are between 5 and 15 minutes long and in that time they must do everything that a feature-length piece would do. We must care about the characters, those characters must face some kind of threat, be in some kind of jeopardy, and we must feel that we, like them, have been on some kind of mental journey by the time we emerge blinking into reality. It's difficult to pull off in 90 minutes and harder still in ten. But if you can produce an interesting ten-minute script, producers are more likely to want to see longer work. And, of course, the internet has made it much easier than ever before to find an outlet for your work. A good film put out on the internet has a chance of gaining a respectable audience as word spreads virally across the web.

Exercise 99

1 Write out your dream cast list for a short film with at least three, but no more than six, characters.
2 Keeping them in mind, write the script for the film.
3 Research five places to send your script to.

Professional tip from Jenny Lecoat

Television is essentially collaborative. No matter how many months you have spent working alone on your script, and no matter how many times you may have rewritten and redrafted it before submission, remember that for the person reading it, it is still a first draft. And, even if that person loves it, there will be many more drafts.

Jenny Lecoat has written for many of the top soap operas in the UK and the USA and has also worked as a stand-up comedian.

10 THINGS TO REMEMBER

1 *There is still a large market for fresh, innovative material.*

2 *Use Final Draft as your screenwriting software (www.finaldraft.com).*

3 *Screenwriting can be very lucrative.*

4 *Comedy is famously hard to write but it opens the most doors.*

5 *Screenwriting is a great opportunity to work with other writers.*

6 *Have specific actors in mind as you write.*

7 *Consider making your own short film.*

8 *'A good script is one that the talent likes' (Nik Powell).*

9 *Expect to do many drafts of your script.*

10 *Think visually.*

19

Agents and publishers

In this chapter you will learn:
- *about the role of an agent and how to find one*
- *about the role of a publisher*
- *about small presses*
- *how to cope with rejection.*

  My agent gets ten per cent of everything I get, except my blinding headaches.

  Fred Allen

How *not* to get published

What happens when you've written your book? Well, you check it carefully for typos, pick a publisher from the *Writers' and Artists' Yearbook* and send it off together with a polite covering letter which more or less approximates to the lyrics of The Beatles' 'Paperback Writer'.

After a few weeks a letter comes back offering you a deal and a huge advance.

A couple of months after that a cheque arrives and with it the beautiful cover. The proofs arrive and you correct them (not that there's much to correct) and some weeks after that the (glowing) reviews are appearing; the book is on the shelves of every high street bookshop in the land; the Chinese translation rights have been sold; Steven Spielberg is making a movie with Johnny Depp in the lead role; and you are swigging back fine wines in discreet city clubs with the cream of the literati. Zadie Smith has got your mobile number and uses it. You're a regular on *Question Time* and *Oprah*; you've just been asked to appear on *Desert Island Discs*; and Ivy League universities are bidding for your manuscripts and letters and shopping lists.

You wish.

The reality is that if you simply send your manuscript off to a publisher you will be placed on the slush pile.

This is a filing cabinet full of manuscripts awaiting the attention of a 17-year-old intern who might, if you are lucky, pass your book on upwards if they feel that it has any merit. The intern might be a gifted and perceptive reader, but they're also going to be very busy answering the phone, ordering paper for the photocopier and making coffee for the more senior executives. They're also very quickly going to suffer from novel fatigue as they try to stay enthusiastic about yet another World War II romance.

Insight

Just sticking your manuscript, however brilliant, into an envelope and punting it off to publishers is not giving it your best shot. It is the equivalent of turning up on a date late, scruffy, unwashed and skint. It shows a lack of respect towards the industry and towards your own work.

In the first instance what you need to do is find an agent.

Why do you need an agent?

Having a good agent is like having a native guide through hostile territory. A good agent is not a counsellor, a social worker, a teacher, an editor, a lawyer, an expert in industrial relations or a psychotherapist, though at times they might seem like all these things. They are not really your mate either, not at first, though with luck they may become one. A good agent is your champion in the publishing world. For 10 or 15 per cent of your earnings, they will try and find the most suitable editor at the publisher best placed to promote your work well.

Having found a publisher they will negotiate fees, often including fees for audio books, film rights and foreign sales. And before all this they will also often do the work that editors used to do but don't really any more. A skilful agent reads your work for its literary merit, but also with their knowledge of the current marketplace. They will make suggestions for ways to improve your manuscript, which are usually worth following. Bear in mind that they like your writing – that's why they took you on in the first place – so what they have to say about your book is made with your best interests as a writer at heart.

The trouble is – like any really good things – they can be hard to find.

Aspiring writers often have negative things to say about agents just as they do about publishing in general. This is probably to do with the arbitrary power they seem to wield. An agent's thumbs down can seem as damning to the new writer as any given by the old Roman emperors in the Colosseum. But generally agents love books. They spend all their time reading books or talking about books or thinking about books. Would they do that if they were really just cynical salespeople? There must be easier ways of making a good living than wading through the literary outpourings of the public. So what if agents want to make money? That's fair enough isn't it? After all, so do you.

Insight

I have to say that, in my experience, if you eavesdrop on a conversation between professional writers they are likely to be talking about money, while two agents are quite likely to be talking about literature.

Having an agent is doubly useful because publishers use them as a filter. If you have succeeded in convincing an agent that there is potential in your book, then publishers are much more likely to take notice.

> **Insight**
> Many publishers – particularly the bigger ones – will only look at work submitted to them via an agent. Agents build up a relationship with editors, so that when editors receive a submission they know that someone they trust thinks it is a book they will like and that will sell.

How do you get an agent?

Writers often go about trying to find agents in the wrong way. They just mail a manuscript to an agency and then hope for the best. Do this and you are probably wasting a stamp.

You want an agent who is going to be sympathetic to your work so it is worth doing some research. First-time novelists will always thank their agents somewhere on the book, so if you have read a first novel you have enjoyed and whose work seems to be in a similar area to yours, then that agent might be a possibility. Use the internet to find out which established writers agents represent. Agents often give talks at literary festivals, so go along and hear what they have to say. Many – most – agents will have a lot of clients that they are already looking after and may just be too busy to give you the attention your work needs. They may not be simply giving you the brush off when they say that their lists are full.

> **Insight**
> With this in mind you should try finding newer agents who are still building a list. You could try phoning the receptionist and finding out who has recently joined the firm.

When you have a list of potential agents don't send them the whole manuscript. Send them the first 60 pages of your book, together with a polite, short covering letter. If they like the opening pages then they'll ask for the rest. Send your pages in a proper jiffy bag. Don't use one of those made from recycled cardboard that will explode in a cloud of grey chaff when your would-be agent tears it open. If you have just ruined a favourite outfit then the agent is unlikely to look upon your work as favourably as they might have done otherwise.

Don't send a synopsis. This is controversial advice, I know. Lots of other people will say you should always send one. What's the point? If they don't like the first 60 pages, they are unlikely to say to themselves, 'but look how it ends'! If they like the pages they'll read the whole book anyway.

Send your work to several agents simultaneously. Again, controversial advice but it means that if one agent rings you up asking to meet, then you can call the others, saying that you are having a meeting with Agent X and could you perhaps meet them too? At the very least this will ensure that they read your work pretty quickly.

Insight

Contrary to popular opinion, agents will always read your work. Of course they will. Every single agent has their own personal nightmare where they turned down J. K. Rowling. Every single one fears going down in history as the next Dick Rowe. (Dick Rowe was the man who turned down The Beatles when he was at Decca Records.) All work gets read properly eventually, so be patient.

WHEN TO CONTACT AN AGENT

It is best to wait until you have finished your book and got it into its best possible shape. This means at least a second, possibly even a third, full draft. If an agent accepts you on the strength of 60 brilliant pages, and the rest of the book is theoretical at this stage, misunderstandings can occur. The book you eventually produce might well be some distance from the book the agent thought you were producing. Cue disappointment all round.

THE COVERING LETTER

This should be short, polite and employ judicious use of flattery, 'I've heard that you are a fantastic agent and you represent X whose work I very much admire...'. Don't write too much about yourself, just that which is interesting. Don't mention your job unless it's a very interesting one or relevant to the book. You are selling yourself as well as the work. Do mention any courses you've taken such as those with the Arvon Foundation. Mention too any successes you have had with writing, prizes won or stories published. If you have a track record then let them know. Don't forget to include your contact details.

Send your letter to a named agent. Simply sending it to the agency will mean that it could end up anywhere, including on the desk of the newest intern. You can follow up with a phone call but wait at least a few weeks before you do this.

Exercise 100

Write a practice covering letter. Make sure that you get it proofread by a competent, literate friend.

MEETING AGENTS

You should, if you get the chance, shop around for agents.
I suppose, I didn't. The first agent I approached agreed to take
me on and I was thrilled. I had met her once before at a literary
event and knew already that she was razor-sharp, hard-working,
thoughtful and passionate about books. She is also incredibly
personable, which is important to me. It might not be to you.
I have a writer friend who prizes his agent because she is, in his
words 'a Rottweiler', a notorious terrorizer of publishers who
generally plays hardball in every aspect of her life. I can see why
you might want that in an agent. It's not for me though. I like to
be able to have a laugh with my agent.

And her comments on my work have always been astute and her
dealings with the business end of things more than professional.
This is not to say that I have always taken her advice. But on those
occasions when I've trusted my judgement rather than hers, I have
always, always been wrong. She has never said 'I told you so' even
though she could have. I wouldn't have blamed her.

Not all agents are as good as this. Anyone can set themselves up
as an agent, which is another reason for doing your research first.
Know who else they represent and meet them in their offices to
decide whether you can trust them.

Publishers

If you keep writing for any length of time you will begin to hear a
lot of moaning about publishers. Some of it is justified. However,
one thing that should keep you from falling prey to a debilitating
despair is the fact that writers have *always* been complaining about
the publishing industry.

It is true that publishers face some difficult times. Reading as a
leisure pursuit is in decline, squeezed by the plethora of noisier

alternatives. The big bookselling chains and the supermarkets demand huge discounts which eat into publishers', already small, profit margin.

Books have a much shorter shelf-life than they once did. If the book doesn't shift copies in the first few weeks, then it is off the shelves and heading back to the warehouse. The carefully crafted books that take a year of agony to write are less in demand than ever before. Instead the ghosted celebrity memoir, fitness bibles, cookbooks and television tie-ins dominate.

Publishers, you will hear it said, are no longer the family-run outfits of a presumed Golden Age (which always seems to be the 1950s, just after the war and just before rock and roll), but instead are mostly part of huge multinationals who care about profits for the shareholders rather than about literature or writing.

SMALL COGS IN A BIG MACHINE

Authors are so many cogs in a machine producing units for mass consumption, and if the masses don't want a serious volume of the units you produce, then let's get somebody else in. Let's try and turn another – preferably young and good-looking – writer into a brand. Better still, let's find an established young and good-looking brand – a pop star or a footballer's girlfriend – and see if we can squeeze some units out of that.

The independent bookshops are all closing, Amazon is selling books with huge discounts, Tesco and Walmart sell them for still less and even libraries have become internet cafés where the loaning out of books is just a sideline to their real business of helping the long-term unemployed brush up their computer skills. All this and worse is what you'll hear and there's some truth to it.

It seems that in the old days writers were allowed to grow and develop, to build a following. Publishers would keep faith with an author over several books, not necessarily making money until quite late on in a writer's career. Not now. These days instant returns are demanded. And even if those instant returns are achieved then they must be equalled with the next book. Even well-established authors live in fear of their books being rejected.

Despite this, publishing houses, like literary agencies, are staffed by people who love books. Really love books, to the point of being obsessed by them. In fact, more books are published in the UK than ever before. The industry still makes money.

Insight

Surprising – and heartwarming – fact: according to an article in a recent *London Review of Books*, the book trade in the UK is worth rather more than the bread industry. Around £9 billion in fact. And the US book industry is still worth $80 billion.

And at least you have the advantage of writing in English. Foreign publishers buy far more books of ours than we do of theirs. Last year, for example, only around 40 of the 100,000 books published in German were translated into English. Even the winner of the German equivalent of the Man Booker prize wasn't published in English.

FRESH TALENT

And publishers still want to find the next big thing. As a new writer you do have one huge advantage over the competition. You are a fresh voice. You are offering something different. If you are a writer on your fourth novel and the last three sold, say, 5,000 each, your publisher could be forgiven for thinking that this one too will sell 5,000 copies. Why should the writer suddenly sell millions now? Whereas a new voice might just catch hold of the public imagination and make mega-bucks for all concerned. The publishing industry needs new writers or there's no industry at all. And yes, of course they are tempted to invest in the young and good-looking, but there are plenty of inspiring stories about older first-time writers. Marina Lewycka (*A Short History of Tractors in Ukrainian*), Alice Sebold (*The Lovely Bones*) and Mary Wesley (*The Camomile Lawn*) had been writing unsuccessfully for years before they were picked up and became household names.

There are still some very big advances being offered to writers. You'll have no doubt read about those in six figures, but these headline figures don't generally stand up to too much scrutiny. Say a writer gets £100,000 ($150,000), this might well be for three books with just one-third paid upon signing. The rest of the money is paid as further books are delivered.

If each book takes, on average, two years from first idea to first print run, then that is actually slightly less than £17,000 ($25,000) per year, a figure which actually compares rather badly with being a nurse or a teacher. And that's for a huge advance; most are much smaller. The average advance for a first novel is about £3,000 ($4,500). J. K. Rowling's first advance was £1,500 ($2,250) paid in two instalments. And if a writer gets a huge advance, then they need huge sales. Should those sales not be forthcoming then they are likely to be dumped with very little ceremony. And who wants to be an ex-novelist?

Some people make a lot of money from books. But I guess it won't be us, not yet anyway. Generally the more a publisher pays for a book, the more they will invest in promoting a book. Authors don't want the big advances just because they're greedy but because they want a publisher to get behind their book with advertising and promotion. Publishers that have invested a lot of hard cash will energize their sales teams; will organize special events; will make sure your books are visible in the shops. (They do this by paying for display space. Independent bookshops will put whoever they want in the window or in prominent piles in the shop. The big chains have sold this space to publishers.)

Small presses

It is true that there are fewer mainstream publishers than ever before (many of the imprints turn out to be owned by the same company), but changes in the printing and distribution industry have meant that there are a lot (really a lot) of small presses, many with very good reputations, which succeed in developing the careers of their writers. Some of these writers are happy to stay with the publishers who discovered them, others move up to the bigger league.

Insight

You could argue that the genuine nurseries for new writing talent are the small independent publishers.

A lot of independent publishers are kitchen table affairs. Book enthusiasts trying to publish half a dozen titles on a shoestring. These are people who only publish books they genuinely like instead of trying to second-guess the marketplace. Because of this, they often score some real surprise successes. Before submitting your book to the small presses however, do them the courtesy of treating them professionally. Make sure you get hold of some of their other titles. Read them. Follow the publisher's submission guidelines carefully.

If you go with a small press it may be unlikely that you'll be able to stroll into your local Waterstone's or Barnes and Noble and see the book on the shelf. But direct sales from publishers are becoming more important, even for the big companies. And the one big advantage of the rise of Amazon is that there now exists a warehouse where readers can get hold of virtually every book that there has ever been. Books stay on the shelves of bookshops for a shorter time than ever before but, paradoxically, they remain available forever.

Coping with rejection

Who knew that the rejections you need are those of the most crushing kind? Nice ones are just too upsetting.

When my agent started sending out my first book she chose eight editors. The responses could be filed into three sets: the brutally dismissive (2), the lukewarm (2) and the heartbreakingly enthusiastic (4). During that whole painful process I discovered the truth that being turned down by someone who says that they 'absolutely loved' the book is far harder to deal with than the ones who give a curt 'this is not for me'. It's because it seems to leave you with nowhere to go. If even the editors that love the book won't put it out, what do you do then?

You write another book, that's what.

If you're at an earlier stage than this and getting rejections from agents or publishers that keep mentioning the same things (lack of pace, too much back story, etc.) then perhaps you need to rework your manuscript once more, addressing these concerns.

You can always console yourself with the thought that J. K. Rowling's book *Harry Potter and The Philosopher's Stone* was turned down by nine publishers, Stephen King was rejected 84 times before publishing his first short story. Robert Pirsig was turned down by a staggering 122 publishers before going on to sell millions of his classic *Zen and the Art of Motorcycle Maintenance*. Even Zadie Smith was rejected by HarperCollins before all her recent successes with Penguin.

Insight

Rejections are a badge of honour, battle scars in the fight to produce your very best work. The desire to prove the critics wrong should spur you on all the more.

Self-publishing

There exist a number of companies who will agree, for a fee, to publish your book. This is known as vanity publishing and something to be avoided unless you are a) very wealthy and b) very self-confident.

You can, of course, become a publisher yourself and control the whole process from editing and cover design, to marketing and distribution. I would avoid this too, except as a last resort.

Part of the desire to be published springs from the need for validation. We need to know if what we have to say is worth hearing. And how can we know that if we have become our own publisher? It is important for your self-esteem as a writer to know that others have invested *their* precious time, talent and energy into your work. Self-publishing feels a little like buying friends to me. Slightly demeaning. And what are you going to do with all those books once they are back from the printers?

Insight

Editing, proofreading and cover design are all specialist tasks that need doing properly and even if you can pay someone to do them for you, getting the books into the shops, getting press reviews, etc. is much harder. It will either take up all your time or the books will sit in your garage in boxes, a silent reproach to you for your impatience. Either way it will stop you doing what you should be doing which is writing the next book.

My only qualification to this would be if you are exceptionally elderly or exceptionally ill and want to leave your writings in a presentable form for your family. When you genuinely just don't have the time to wait for publishers to discover you.

Professional tip from Camilla Hornby

Agents and publishers are people too, just busy people, so make your approach concise and literate and make the material as good as it can be before sending it in.

Camilla Hornby is an agent at Curtis Brown.

10 THINGS TO REMEMBER

1 *Agents do care about books.*

2 *Agents will – in the end – read everything.*

3 *Publishers will usually only look at work submitted via an agent.*

4 *Only send work to an agent when it is as polished as you can make it.*

5 *Send an agent the first 60 pages of your book, rather than the whole manuscript.*

6 *Make sure you've finished your book before approaching agents.*

7 *Send your work to a named agent.*

8 *Send your work in a proper jiffy bag, double-spaced, with writing on only one side of the paper.*

9 *Many of the most exciting writers are published by small, independent publishers.*

10 *Without new writers there is no publishing industry. Keep going.*

20

Moving on

In this chapter you will learn:
- *about the writing community*
- *where to find creative writing courses*
- *about literary festivals.*

> *The only sensible ends of literature are, first, the pleasurable toil of writing; second, the gratification of one's family and friends; and, lastly the solid cash.*
>
> Nathaniel Hawthorne

Creative writing classes

If you have enjoyed the exercises in this book you will be feeling more confident in your writing than you were a few weeks or months ago. Perhaps you have some poems or short stories that feel finished and that you are happy with. Perhaps you have sent some off to competitions. Maybe you have a novel developing, or a play or a screenplay. You will definitely have a notebook bulging with ideas.

If you have managed some of this on your own then you have proved that you have the true writer's ability to deal with solitude. You have self-discipline and perseverance and these are the two most important qualities you need as a writer.

Calvin Coolidge once said,

Nothing in this world can take the place of persistence.
Talent will not; nothing is more common than unsuccessful
people with talent. Genius will not; unrewarded genius is
almost a proverb. Education will not; the world is full of
educated derelicts. Persistence and determination alone are
omnipotent. The slogan 'press on' has solved and always
will solve the problems of the human race.

Insight

There is a writing community, and feeling yourself to be a
part of that wider world can make the business of writing –
the business of perseverance – seem less painful. Yes, writing
is something you do largely on your own, but there is a
family of writers too.

Creative writing classes can help you develop your skills more
quickly, as you also learn from your fellow classmates' successes and
failures. There was a time when local authorities ran evening classes
in almost everything and creative writing would definitely be on the
curriculum somewhere. These classes seem very much geared to the
world of work these days, and so finding those which develop the
spirit, or what Ted Hughes called 'the imagination of the tribe', seems
harder than it was. Nevertheless, some enlightened councils still offer
creative writing classes and it's worth contacting the arts or culture
department of your council to find out if they are running them.
The public library should also have details of courses in your area.

The Workers Educational Association (WEA) also runs classes of
all kinds and very often creative writing is part of their programme.
The WEA courses are also very inexpensive.

The Arvon Foundation

I've referred to Arvon several times in the course of this book. This
is not just because I run one of the centres, but because the Arvon

formula really works. Set up by poets John Moat and John Fairfax in 1968, an Arvon course sees up to 16 students working with two professional writers for five days. The alchemy of workshops, discussions, readings, one-to-one feedback, being surrounded by other writers, and no distractions, really does push students to make giant strides with their writing. A third professional writer comes as the midweek guest reader to provide yet another positive element to the mix.

The list of tutors who have worked for Arvon is hugely impressive. Novelists such as Stan Barstow, Suzanne Berne, Mavis Cheek, Jill Dawson, Suzannah Dunn, Kathryn Heyman, Hanif Kureishi, Deborah Levy, Toby Litt, Thomas Lynch, Caryl Phillips, Will Self, Sarah Waters and Edmund White have all worked with Arvon recently. All the leading contemporary poets including Simon Armitage, Carol Ann Duffy, Daljit Nagra, Hugo Williams, and many others, have worked at Arvon. Also, playwrights such as Willy Russell and Simon Stephens; television writers like Jimmy McGovern; and film directors like Anthony Minghella.

Insight

I'm sure the secret of Arvon's success is the sense of purposeful, creative endeavour and good fellowship that a week spent writing without worrying about work, children, spouses or any of the daily grind, engenders. And no distractions really does mean just that. There is no internet, no email, no television, no radio; just good company in a beautiful setting.

Arvon has created brilliant writers too: Booker Prize winner Pat Barker started writing on an Arvon course, as did the prize-winning novelist Lesley Glaister, as well as well-known poets like Neil Rollinson, Carole Satyamurti and Michael Laskey.

You will find that friendships formed with your fellow students provide you with constructive candid readers, and supportive relationships that will sustain you through years of writing.

You can find out about Arvon's courses at www.arvonfoundation.org, or phone 020 7931 7611, or write for a brochure to:

The Arvon Foundation
The Free Word Centre
60 Farringdon Road
London EC1R 3oA

SCOTLAND AND WALES

Similar operations to Arvon are run at Ty Newydd in Wales, and Moniack Mhor in Scotland, which provide a range of exciting courses for writers at all levels. These include courses for those who want to write in Welsh or in Gaelic. Both houses are historic and in beautiful locations. Moniack Mhor is in the most evocative part of the Highlands, close to Loch Ness, while Ty Newydd is on the Welsh coast at Cricieth and is the former home of Lloyd George.

For details of their courses write to:

Ty Newydd
Llanstumdwy
Cricieth
Gwynedd LL52 oLW
Tel: 01766 522811
Email: post@tynewdd.org
Website: www.tynewydd.org

Moniack Mhor Writer's Centre
Teavarran
Kiltarlity
Inverness-shire IV4 7HT
Tel: 01463 741 675
Email: m-mhor@arvonfoundation.org
Website: www.moniackmhor.org.uk

Literary festivals and conferences

Literary festivals are great places to see and hear your favourite writers, and to find out about the great writers of the future. As well as talks and readings by writers, many literary festivals run workshops and master-classes in which you can participate.

Conferences too are places where writers gather and, in addition to the useful lectures and workshops, many important writing friendships can be formed at mealtimes and in the bar.

Writers' circles

You might want to join a writers' circle (they can have other names). The idea behind a writers' circle is that you read one another's work (presumably sitting in a circle) in turn. It gives you a chance to have your work read, or heard, by other writers who will provide valuable feedback.

When looking for a writers' circle there are several things to consider.

FREQUENCY OF MEETINGS

If you are looking for feedback then you want a group that meets regularly and frequently and one that goes on meeting through the summer holidays.

VENUE

Private houses are not the best venues for writers' circles, as they encourage chat rather than serious discussion of writing. Ideally your group should meet on neutral ground such as a school or a library. Otherwise it is too much of a social occasion.

Different groups have different rules about feedback. In an ideal world every writers' circle would give plenty of time for discussion of manuscripts and that discussion would be frank but never discouraging. You will need a good chairperson who will ensure everyone gets the airtime they need and that the meetings aren't dominated by the same garrulous voices every week.

Insight

I think these kinds of groups work best when they consider just one or two chunks of manuscript at a session. These extracts should have been circulated in advance so that those commenting on them can read them properly rather than being expected to respond on a first hearing or a cursory read. People whose works are being discussed should not be allowed to contribute to the discussion until the end when everyone else has had their say.

This may seem unduly harsh, but it means that the writer is forced to listen to the whole debate about their work without getting defensive or trying to explain complicated plot points. It allows those giving the feedback to talk freely, knowing that the author isn't going to jump down their throat.

Each circle will have its own way of doing things, but a good one will let you sit in for a few evenings to see if it is for you. Most of these groups charge a small subscription for membership.

The creative writing MA

Not so long ago there were only a couple of these in the UK. In the USA they are much more established. Most people know of the one at University of East Anglia set up by Malcolm Bradbury (though it wasn't the first, that honour goes to Lancaster University), but there are now over 100 in the UK.

Most universities now offer a creative writing MA to those with a first degree in any discipline. All of the universities will have some kind of entrance criteria. This may be a request to look at your work, or an interview, or both. Most universities offer both full-time and part-time courses. In 2010 the fees for this MA were around £3,500.

These are most useful for the concentrated time they allow you to write, and for the support and solidarity you will get from other students. The support you get from the tutors varies of course. Many great writers are not necessarily great teachers. Others may not do all that much teaching anyway, their presence in a university being mainly symbolic. Often the universities who have the best creative departments are not those with the most famous writers as their tutors, but those staffed by working writers with a genuine commitment to helping their students to progress.

Insight

With so many of these courses there is no longer the expectation that all the students will move seamlessly from completing their MA to publication. Most students who successfully obtain degrees will not become published authors, and it is as well to know this before you begin.

THE DISTANCE LEARNING MA

I have an MA from Manchester Metropolitan University and I followed an online course which gave me the chance to study from home. I 'met' my fellow students in a university-hosted chat room once a week where we critiqued the work of two of our peers. These sessions were hosted by professional tutors. In addition there was a programme of reading as well as academic work marked by the lecturers.

It was fascinating. It was helpful to my own writing because the other students were both fair and candid in their appraisals of my work, but it was also interesting because I got the chance to talk regularly with literature enthusiasts from all over the world. There were students based in Canada, Nigeria, Dubai, Belgium, Germany, New York and Borneo, as well as those of us in less glamorous locations such as West Yorkshire.

There were many fine writers among them and several who I am still in touch with. There was a better hit rate than most from that course in that four of us went on to be published within a year of the course finishing. Online study has its disadvantages (lack of personal contact, doesn't get you away from the computer screen), but I found the mixture of students' backgrounds, interests and ages exhilarating.

Another good online MA is the one run by Lancaster University. The poets Graham Mort and Paul Farley preside over a course which is well run and well respected.

I expect that in years to come many more similar internet-based courses will begin to appear.

UNDERGRADUATE DEGREES AND DIPLOMAS

Universities and colleges are now beginning to offer courses for those who do not already have a degree and perhaps this will be more suitable for you. Degree courses are generally three years (full time) and several have creative writing as a component with other arts subjects, such as English or Film Studies. Diploma courses tend to be shorter.

Literary consultancies

There are a number of organizations now which will offer professional critiques of your work for a fee. Quite a few writers now top up their incomes by offering this service, while others work for established consultancies. The best known is also the oldest: The Literary Consultancy (see 'Taking it further') was founded in 1996 and has a very good reputation for using highly qualified writers to offer comprehensive candid feedback within a reasonably short timeframe. Others may not be so reputable. It is always worth finding other writers who have used the services of a particular consultancy, before committing any money. At the time of writing, fees for recognized consultancies work out at about £1 for a page of critiqued work. Or £300 ($450) or so to get rigorous feedback on a complete novel.

The award-winning writer Jill Dawson helps organize Gold Dust, which offers mentoring as well as feedback on writing. Several other quite well-known writers also offer similar services privately.

There are numerous other very reputable literary consultancies and you can find their addresses in the *Writers' and Artists' Yearbook*.

Mentoring

I remember Hanif Kureishi saying once that it was impossible for any writer to break through on their own. Everyone, however gifted, needs guidance through the process. Mentoring of this sort has become far more commonplace now, and if you are serious about developing your writing then you will be encouraged to become involved in this process.

Gold Dust is one writer-led mentoring programme that provides a number of one-to-one sessions with highly respected professionals, in addition to a personalized feedback service. There are other private initiatives of this sort, but there are charitable ones too such as those organized by the Jerwood Foundation, and several schemes organized by Arts Council England. The Arts Council will occasionally support new writers who wish to purchase the services of established writers to work with them and it is always worth building a relationship with your regional

Literature Officer. (See 'Taking it further' for more information on these organizations.)

London writers may find organizations such as Spread The Word and Apples and Snakes useful. Both of these organizations are, like the Arvon Foundation, based in the new Free Word Centre, an Arts Council funded 'Ministry of Literature' in the old Guardian newsroom in the centre of the City.

Congratulations! You have finished the course... Well done. There isn't a certificate to give you, but then writing is not about certificates. Nor is it about awards, prizes, honorary degrees or smiley faces at the bottom of the page. Writing is about making the world intelligible for yourself and for others. And it's about entertainment. It's about giving your readers something they can't get anywhere else.

10 THINGS TO DO NOW

1 *Write for ten minutes. Yes, right now.*

2 *Find a regular time in your daily schedule when you can write.*

3 *Join a writers' group.*

4 *Look up the Arvon Foundation website (or order the brochure).*

5 *Tell everyone you know that you are a writer. Get them to take you seriously.*

6 *Explore writing courses at your local college or university.*

7 *Make contact with your nearest Arts Centre and find out about live literature events.*

8 *Compare your most recent piece of writing with the very first things you wrote.*

9 *Congratulate yourself on your progress. Have some cake, a biscuit or a beer. Buy yourself something.*

10 *Read a book.*

I've said it before, I'll say it again: make sure you always have a notebook.

Taking it further

Organizations

The Arvon Foundation
Free Word Centre
60 Farringdon Road
London EC1R 3GA
Tel: 020 7324 2554
Website: www.arvonfoundation.org

Gold Dust
PO Box 247
Ely CB7 9BX
Website: www.gold-dust.org.uk

Send three chapters and brief synopsis of the work in progress (novel, stories or life-writing) and your name, address and email address.

The Jerwood Foundation
22 Fitzroy Square
London W1T 6EN
Tel: 020 7388 6287
Fax: 020 7388 6289
Email: info@jerwood.org
Website: www.jerwood.org

Arts Council England
There are nine regional offices each with a Literature Officer.
Phone for details.
Tel: 0845 300 6200
Textphone: 020 7973 6564
Website: www.artscouncil.org.uk

Scottish Arts Council
12 Manor Place
Edinburgh EH3 7DD
Tel: 0131 226 6051
Website: www.scottisharts.org.uk

Arts Council of Wales
Bute Place
Cardiff CF10 5AL
Tel: 0845 8734 900
Website: www.artswales.org.uk

Arts Council of Northern Ireland
77 Malone Road
Belfast BT9 6AQ
Tel: +44 (28) 90385200
Website: www.artscouncil-ni.org

The Poetry Society
22 Betterton Street
London WC2H 9BX
Tel: 020 7420 9880
Website: www.poetrysociety.org.uk

The Literary Consultancy Ltd
Free Word Centre
60 Farringdon Road
London EC1R 3GA
Tel: 020 7324 2563
Email: info@literaryconsultancy.co.uk
Website: www.literaryconsultancy.co.uk

Bibliography

Where books are still available for purchase, details of the
latest edition are given – sources www.amazon.com and
www.bookdepository.co.uk.

If a book is no longer easily available a search has been made on
the internet to assess second-hand availability using the search
engine of Abebooks – www.abebooks.com.

Where a book has proved difficult to locate through usual retail
outlets and the second-hand market the entry has been marked
'Check with the library'.

Allen, Walter, (ed.), *Writers on Writing* (London: Phoenix House
and New York: E. P. Dutton, 1948). Words about writing by
some of the world's greatest writers. Both poetry and the novel
are covered. Available second-hand via the internet.

Allott, Miriam, *Novelists on the Novel* (London and Boston:
Routledge and Kegan Paul, 1960). Includes quotes from Hardy,
Fielding, Dickens, Zola, Trollope, Tolstoy and many others.
Available second-hand via the internet.

Archer, William, *Playmaking: A Manual of Craftmanship* (London:
Chapman and Hall, 1959). Reissued 2009 by University of
Michigan Library. Available via the internet.

Armstrong, David, *How Not To Write A Novel* (London: Allison
and Busby, 2003). Essential reading for anyone contemplating
writing a novel. Funny, wise and true.

Ash, William, *The Way to Write Radio Drama* (reissue, London:
Elm Tree Books, 1985). Radio drama techniques including plot,
theme, character and dialogue. Also covers what happens when
a script is accepted for broadcast.

Baker, Donna, *How to Write Stories for Magazines* (revised edition, London: Allison and Busby, 1995). Check with the library.

Baldwin, Michael, *The Way to Write Poetry* (reissue, London: Elm Tree Books, 1982). Check with the library.

Bates, H. E., *The Modern Short Story* (London: Michael Joseph, 1982). A critical survey of the short story. Available second-hand via the internet.

Bird, Carmel, *Dear Writer* (London: Virago Press, 1990). A classic guide to writing fiction. Available second-hand via the internet.

Braine, John, *Writing a Novel* (London: Eyre Methuen), reissued as *How to Write a Novel* (London: Methuen, 1974). John Braine was both a novelist and book reviewer. This practical handbook is considered by many to be a classic guide to the art of writing a novel.

Brande, Dorothea, *Becoming a Writer* (new edition, London: Macmillan, 1996). Originally published in 1934 by Pan. Writing techniques and exercises plus how to find the 'writer's magic'.

Brewer's Theatre (London: Weidenfeld & Nicolson, 1994). A phrase and fable dictionary devoted exclusively to the theatre. Available second-hand via the internet.

Chisholm, Alison, *The Craft of Writing Poetry* (2nd edition, London: Allison and Busby, 1998). A second revised and updated edition which provides basic and practical advice for aspiring poets, from first idea to final revision.

Cooke, Brian, *Writing Comedy for Television* (London: Methuen, 1983). Available second-hand via the internet.

Cooper, Giles, *Radio Plays* (London: BBC Publications, 1982). Distinguished plays from authors such as Jeremy Sandford, C. P. Taylor and Alan Sharpe. Available second-hand via the internet.

Corner, Helen and Weatherly, Lee, *Write a Blockbuster And Get it Published* (London: Hodder Education, 2010). An indispensable guide for anyone who wants to write commercial fiction.

Derrick, Christopher, *Reader's Report* (London: Victor Gollancz, 1969). A publisher's reader gives the aspiring author advice on the pitfalls of submission. Available second-hand via the internet.

Dick, Jill, *Freelance Writing for Newspapers* (3rd edition, London: A & C Black, 2003). Brought up to date to include selling to internet publishers, and covering topics from approaching a news editor to selling rights.

Dick, Jill, *Writing for Magazines* (2nd edition, London: A & C Black, 1996). Writing and selling non-fiction to magazines, including interviewing and a section on electronic aids for the magazine writer.

Dipple, Elizabeth, *Plot* (London: Methuen, 1977). Available second-hand via the internet.

Dorner, Jane, *The Internet: A Writer's Guide* (2nd edition, London: A & C Black, 2001). A comprehensive guide for beginners and experts alike.

Dorner, Jane, *Writing on Disk* (London: John Taylor Book Ventures, 1992). Check with the library.

Doubtfire, Dianne, *The Craft of Novel-Writing* (revised edition, London: Allison and Busby, 1998).

Fairfax, John, and Moat, John, *The Way to Write* (Penguin Books, 1998). A practical guide for beginners which explains how to evaluate and improve your work.

Finch, Peter, *How to Publish your Poetry* (4th edition, London and New York: Allison and Busby, 1998). Essential topics for the would-be published poet.

Forster, E. M., *Aspects of the Novel* (new edition, Penguin Books, 2000). How to see through novels, not round them. A critical revision of the text by Oliver Stallybrass has given this much-quoted title a new lease of life.

Fountain, Tim, *How to Write a Play* (London: Nick Hern Books, 2007). Clear and sensible advice on the art of playwriting.

Frankau, Pamela, *Pen to Paper* (London: Heinemann, 1961). A novelist's notebook. Available second-hand via the internet.

Friedman, Rosemary, *The Writing Game* (London: Empiricus Books, 1999). A thoughtful and revealing exploration of creative writing.

Goldberg, Natalie, *Writing Down the Bones* (London: Shambhala Press, 1993). Encouragement and advice on many aspects of the writer's craft from an off-beat and refreshing standpoint.

Goldman, William, *Adventures in the Screen Trade* (Abacus, 1996). A personal yet practical view of screenwriting.

Griffiths, Stuart, *How Plays Are Made* (London: Heinemann, 1982). A guide to the basic principles of drama with a focus on structure.

Herbert, John, *Radio Journalism* (London: A & C Black, 1976). Gathering, editing and presenting material for broadcasting. Available second-hand via the internet.

Hines, John, *The Way to Write Non-Fiction* (London: Elm Tree Books, 1990). Researching, writing and selling non-fiction books, market research, writing synopses, finding subject and publisher. Available second-hand via the internet.

Hoffmann, Ann, *Research for Writers* (London: Writing Handbooks, 1999). A research guide for writers and journalists offering practical advice on organization and methods of research.

Hughes, Ted, *The Letters of Ted Hughes*, edited by Christopher Reid (London: Faber and Faber, 2007). Some terrific advice for writers as well as much else of interest to the general reader.

Kitchen, Paddy, *The Way to Write Novels* (reissue, London: Elm Tree Books, 1981). A complete guide to the basic skills of good writing. Available second-hand via the internet.

Krailing, Tessa, *How to Write for Children* (London: Allison and Busby, 1996). How to find inspiration and get new ideas on writing for children of all age groups.

Kuroff, Barbara, (ed.), *Novel and Short Story Writer's Market* (Writer's Digest Books, F & W Publications, USA, 1999). A guide to US markets, publishers, agents, contests, conferences and awards.

Legat, Michael, *The Nuts and Bolts of Writing* (London: Robert Hale, 1989). Available second-hand via the internet.

Legat, Michael, *Plotting the Novel* (London: Robert Hale, 1992). Available second-hand via the internet.

Legat, Michael, *The Writer's Rights* (London: Books for Writers, 1995). A comprehensive guide to the legalities and business of being a published writer.

Legat, Michael, *Writing for Pleasure and Profit* (London: Robert Hale, 1993). Comprehensive guide for beginners.

Long, Rob, *Set Up, Joke, Set Up, Joke* (London: Bloomsbury, 2005). A riveting – and hilarious – guide to the workings of the television industry.

Martin, Rhona, *Writing Historical Fiction* (2nd edition, London: A & C Black, 1995). Different kinds of historical fiction are covered including: the family saga, the romance, the nostalgia novel, the adventure story and the 'straight' historical.

Maurois, André, *The Art of Writing* (London: Bodley Head, and New York: Arno Press, 1960). European men of letters, including Voltaire, Tolstoy, Stendhal, Goethe and Flaubert. Available second-hand via the internet.

Morley, David, *The Cambridge Introduction to Creative Writing* (Cambridge: Cambridge University Press Essays, 2007). Introduces students to the practice and art of creative writing.

Nivison, Kate, *How to Turn Your Holiday into Popular Fiction* (London: Allison and Busby, 1994). Check with the library.

Paice, Eric, *The Way to Write for Television* (reissued revised edition, London: Elm Tree Books, 1987). A complete guide to the basic skills of writing television drama. Available second-hand via the internet.

Phythian, B. A., *Correct English* (revised edition, London: Hodder Education, 2010). A practical guide and reference to improve the use of English in everyday life.

Phythian, B. A., *Essential English Grammar* (revised edition, London: Hodder Education, 2010). Chapters deal with the nature and function of all principal parts of speech and sentence structure. The exercises and tests provided reinforce learning.

Priestley, J. B., *The Art of the Dramatist* (London: William Heinemann Education, 1973). The Inaugural Lecture, under the Hubert Henry Davies fund, given at the Old Vic Theatre on 30 September 1956 together with appendices and discursive notes. Available second-hand via the internet.

Ray, R. J., and Norris, Bret, *The Weekend Novelist* (London: A & C Black, 2005). A 52-week programme to help the writer produce a finished novel.

Rodger, Ian, *Radio Drama* (London: Macmillan, 1981). Available second-hand via the internet.

Sansom, Peter, *Writing Poems* (London: Bloodaxe Books, 1994). Analysis, techniques and writing games, also metre rhyme, half-rhyme, free verse and given forms.

Saunders, Jean, *The Craft of Writing Romance* (London: Writers' Bookshop, 2000).

Saunders, Jean, *Writing Step by Step* (London: Allison and Busby, 1989). Check with the library.

Smethurst, William, *How to Write for Television* (London: How to Books, 2000). Information and advice on all areas of writing for TV. Revised edition includes a rewritten chapter on opportunities for new writers, plus a section on internet help sites and workshops.

Smith, Cathy, *How to Write and Sell Travel Articles* (London: Allison and Busby, 1992). Check with the library.

Steinbeck, John, *Journal of a Novel* (Penguin Books, 2001). A collection of letters forms a day-by-day account of Steinbeck's writing of *East of Eden*, his longest and most ambitious novel.

Stillman, Frances, *The Poet's Manual* (London: Thames and Hudson, 2000). A rhyming dictionary. This volume allows writers to find easily the rhymes they need.

Strunk, William, and White, E. B., *The Elements of Style* (4th edition, Boston: Allyn and Bacon, 1999). Offers advice on improving writing skills and promoting a style marked by simplicity, orderliness and sincerity.

Trewin, Ion, *Journalism* (London: David and Charles, 1975). Available second-hand via the internet.

Truss, Lynne, *Eats, Shoots and Leaves: The Zero Tolerance Approach to Punctuation* (London: Profile, 2007).

Vallins, G. H., *Better English* (London: Pan Books, 1955). Expands on the principles of clear writing and also deals with idiom, figure, the logical expressions of thought and the finer points of language. Available second-hand via the internet.

Vallins, G. H., *Good English* (London: Pan Books, (1964). How to achieve a good, simple English style, whether for reports and stories or for business letters. Available second-hand via the internet.

Wells, Gordon, *The Craft of Writing Articles* (2nd edition, London: Allison and Busby, 1996). A practical guide to writing feature articles and how to sell them.

Wells, Gordon, *How to Write Non-Fiction Books* (London: Writers' Bookshop, 1999). A step-by-step guide to writing and marketing a non-fiction book.

Wells, Gordon, *The Magazine Writer's Handbook* (London: Allison and Busby, 1985) and with McCallum, Chris, *The Magazine Writer's Handbook* (9th revised edition, London: Writers' Bookshop, 2002). For all magazine writers – detailed information on many British magazines and comments on many more.

Wells, Gordon, *Writers' Questions Answered* (London: Allison and Busby Writers' Guides, 2001). For beginners and more experienced writers alike – provides useful information addressing many of the problems that can beset writers.

Whitelaw, Stella, *How to Write and Sell a Book Proposal* (London: Writers' Bookshop, 2000). An informative and entertaining guide to writing synopses and proposals.

Wibberley, Mary, *To Writers With Love* (London: Buchan and Enright, 1993). A helpful guide to writing romance novels.

Writers' and Artists' Yearbook (London: A & C Black, 2007).

Index

Image credits